The Easy Cook
for a busy lifestyle

Edited by Frances Hutchison

Bay Books
Sydney and London

A NOTE ABOUT MEASUREMENTS

Measurements given in cups throughout this book refer to the standard metric cup, which holds 250ml or 8fl oz.

1984 published by Bay Books Pty Ltd
61–69 Anzac Parade
Kensington NSW 2011
© 1984 Bay Books
National Library of Australia
Card Number and ISBN 0 85835 553 1
Photography on pages 15, 33, 40, 44, 52 and 79 by Ashley Barber

Contents

Potato and celery salad

Introduction	5
Soups, sauces and garnishes	6
Starters and snacks	18
Fish and shellfish	28
Meat	36
Poultry	54
Vegetable dishes and salads	62
Pasta and rice	72
Desserts	84
Index	96

Introduction

MOST people today cannot spend hours preparing elaborate meals. Simple, high quality meals prepared from nutritious ingredients and served attractively are the aim of many modern cooks. This book places much emphasis on dishes which are easy to prepare, so it should become an invaluable addition to the cookbook shelf.

With modern dietary trends in mind *The Easy Cookbook* contains chapters covering a wide variety of salads and vegetable dishes, some of which could be a meal in themselves. Also, in response to the needs of busy lifestyles, this book contains a selection of sauces and garnishes which can add flavour and zest to the simplest dish.

Dishes which are simple to prepare are often those which allow the natural flavour of the food to emerge. We are fortunate in having an abundance of high-quality fresh food, including a large variety of delicious fish, year-round fruit and vegetables from cold-climate and tropical areas, and some of the best meat in the world. They are all there for the discerning shopper.

The ingredients used in all of these recipes are readily available and where possible the use of fresh foods is recommended. However a well-stocked pantry is an advantage and some most imaginative dishes can be prepared for unexpected guests if a few staple items are always at hand.

Many recipes include handy tips for easy methods, or variations which extend the scope of the dish. There are recipes for every occasion, from a simple snack to a spectacular dinner party. Complicated procedures have been avoided and practical methods have been favoured throughout.

All measurements are given in metric units; celsius temperatures are followed by fahrenehit equivalents in brackets. The number of servings is stated at the end of each recipe.

The kitchen equipment you use does not need to be elaborate but some basic items such as a set of sharp knives and adequate measuring equipment are important. The multi-purpose food processors which are now available can help you with blending, mixing, slicing and shredding, or juice extracting. Some of the recipes included here are particularly suited to quick preparation using an electric appliance and this is pointed out in the introduction to the recipe. For example, with a blender you can whip up sauces, soups, drinks and desserts within minutes.

The electric frypan is very versatile too: it may be used for roasting, braising, stewing, casseroling, steaming and boiling, as well as frying. There are also special slow cookers, ideal for cooks who are away from home during the day. Food cooked by this method retains its nutrients and flavour and an enjoyable evening meal is ready without fuss.

Larger appliances such as the microwave oven and the freezer can also save a lot of time for the busy cook. If you want to cook meals ahead and then freeze them until needed, remember that it is best to slightly undercook dishes that are to be frozen. This prevents overcooking during the reheating process.

The recipes in this book combine the imagination and experience of the best European cooking with a practical straightforward approach — traditional cooking which has been adapted to the busy lifestyle of the 1980's.

Farmhouse potato and chicken casserole (See page 55)

Soups, sauces and garnishes

SOUP is practically unlimited in its variety; there are wonderfully tasty soups for all occasions — hearty, warming potages for cold winter days, clear flavourful consommés to serve with sherry before a rich main course and refreshing chilled concoctions such as lettuce soup for warm summer evenings. They key to a successful soup is good, fresh ingredients; and if you use as a base a home made stock which has had slow and lengthy cooking, you will be rewarded by greatly improved flavour. Most of us use ready-made stock cubes at some time, but they are highly seasoned and very salty, so exercise care when adding seasonings.

It is possible to make an economic household stock, largely using whatever is to hand, a veal or chicken base for light-coloured soups and sauces, and a brown beef base for consommé, dark soups, sauces, and gravy. A fish base will make a simple fish stock.

Unlike soups, to which almost anything can be added, stock must be clear — vital when making consommé or aspic — so avoid using starchy foods or thickened liquids, which will turn it cloudy. A really concentrated bone stock will set as a firm jelly.

Stock with the surface fat on it may be kept in the refrigerator for a couple of days or it can be frozen if well strained.

A full-bodied stock is the basis of many good dishes including sauces, which can add piquancy to simple plain food without drowning the natural flavour. The classic rich French sauces such as Hollandaise and Béarnaise and simple, tasty vegetable sauces such as tomato are among the most versatile and easy to make. Excellent sauces can also be made by adding a little wine, stock or cream to the juices of meat or fish after it has been cooked.

Bouquet garni

Many soup recipes call for the use of a bouquet garni, the French name for a small bunch of herbs, either fresh or dried, used to flavour dishes. The traditional bouquet garni is made up of a bay leaf, a sprig or two of parsley and thyme, and a few peppercorns, all tied in a small piece of cheesecloth.

It does not matter too much which herbs are used so long as they are aromatic, so you can experiment with different mixtures, incorporating herbs such as chervil, basil, rosemary and tarragon.

Sometimes ready-made bouquets garni in paper sachets are available but these tend to disintegrate with long cooking.

Soup garnishes

Herbs and greens: Finely chop herbs, green celery leaves, chives or the green stems of spring onions and sprinkle over soup.

Bacon: Crumble crisp-fried rashers and sprinkle over soup.

Pasta: Cook either in the soup towards the end of cooking or separately and add before serving.

Croûtes: Remove crusts from slices of French bread, spread with butter (flavoured if liked) or grated cheese on one side and bake until crisp and golden.

Croûtons: Remove crusts from slices of bread, cut into cubes and either fry in hot oil until golden and crisp, or toast.

Melba toast: Remove crusts from slices of white bread. Toast until pale brown then cut through the middle of each to produce extra-thin slices. Toast again, white side up, until golden or bake the thinly cut slices in the bottom of a slow oven until very crisp and curled. Brown under grill.

Sippets: Remove crusts from slices of bread, cut into large triangles and bake in a slow oven until dry and very crisp.

Dumplings or meatballs: Add these either plain or flavoured to the soup towards the end of cooking and simmer for about 20 minutes.

Mushrooms: Thinly slice and gently fry in butter for 5 minutes until soft but not coloured. Sprinkle over the soup just before serving.

Basic household stock

1 kg raw or cooked meat bones, chopped
1 onion
1 carrot
1 stalk celery (optional)
2 litres cold water
1 bouquet garni
1 teaspoon salt
6 peppercorns

Wash the bones. Peel, wash, and roughly chop the onion and carrot. Wash and chop the celery.

Put the bones in a large saucepan, add water, bring to the boil and remove any scum that rises to the surface.

Add the chopped vegetables, bouquet garni and seasonings to the pan. Reduce heat and simmer, covered, for about 4 hours.

Strain the stock and leave to cool. When cold remove the fat from the surface.

This makes about 1.5 litres of stock.

Note: Additions to this stock can include tomato paste, meat trimmings and leftovers (but not liver), bacon rinds, and cooked ham bones.

Fresh tomato soup (See page 13)

Giblet gravy

450 g giblets (excluding liver) chicken or turkey
1 tablespoon vinegar
salt
1 tablespoon tomato paste
1.5 L water
1 bouquet garni
2 stock cubes
few crushed peppercorns

Thickening:
4 tablespoons cornflour
4 tablespoons arrowroot
⅝ cup water
¼ teaspoon gravy browning (optional)

Wash and clean the giblets thoroughly. Soak them in cold water with the vinegar and 1 teaspoon salt. After 1 hour this will draw out the blood. Wash and drain, cover with fresh cold water and bring to the boil. Boil for 5 minutes. Drain and refresh in cold water. Drain again.

Place the giblets in a 2-litre saucepan with the tomato paste, water and bouquet garni and simmer for 1 hour. Crumble the stock cubes into the gravy and season with crushed peppercorns and salt to taste.

Make the thickening by mixing the cornflour, arrowroot and water to a paste in a bowl, then stir this mixture into the boiling gravy. Cook, stirring for 5 minutes until the gravy is clear. Strain the sauce through a fine sieve and add the gravy browning, if necessary, to improve the colour. This makes about 1 litre of gravy.

French onion soup

240 g onions
1 clove garlic
3 tablespoons butter
2 tablespoons flour
1 litre of beef stock
240 mL dry white wine
salt and pepper
4 rounds cut from a French loaf
120 g cheese, grated
1 tablespoon chopped parsley

Peel and chop the onions. Peel and crush the garlic.

Melt half the butter in a sauté pan, add the onions and cook until golden. Add the flour and stir with a wooden spoon until it browns.

Add stock and wine, mixing in well. Add the crushed garlic and cook for about 40 minutes. Adjust seasoning.

While the soup is cooking, toast the bread in a slow oven until very crisp.

Ladle the soup into flameproof bowls. Butter the toast, put one slice in each bowl and liberally sprinkle with the grated cheese. Melt the cheese by placing bowls under a hot grill for a few moments. Serve immediately sprinkled with the chopped parsley.

Serves 4

Note: A heartier version of this soup can be made by adding a lightly poached egg to each dish before the toast.

Beef and carrot soup

1 small onion
½ kg carrots
1 medium potato
3 tablespoons butter
½ teaspoon salt
black pepper, freshly ground
½ teaspoon sugar
700 mL brown stock
1 tablespoon chopped parsley
1 teaspoon chopped chervil or marjoram

Peel and chop the onion; peel and dice the carrots and potato.

Melt the butter in a heavy saucepan and add the onion, carrots and potato. Add the salt, pepper, and sugar. Cover the pan and cook over a low heat for 15 minutes.

Add stock and bring to the boil. Lower heat, cover the pan and cook for a further 15 minutes. Rub the soup through a sieve, or purée in a blender.

Reheat and serve sprinkled with the finely chopped herbs.

Serves 6

Mulligatawny

Created in the days of the British in India, this soup is basically a rich meat stock flavoured with curry and can be made with any meat.

500 g lean breast of lamb
1 large onion
1 medium carrot
1 small green tart apple
2 tablespoons oil
1 tablespoon curry powder
2 tablespoons flour
1¼ litres brown stock
¾ cup milk
1 teaspoon arrowroot
1 tablespoon cold water
salt

Wipe and trim lamb of excess fat; cut into 1 cm wide strips. Peel and slice the onion and carrot; peel, core and slice the apple.

Heat the oil in a large pan. When hot, brown the lamb all over. Take out and add the sliced vegetables and apple and cook, stirring, for about 5 minutes. Stir in the curry powder and cook for a further 2 minutes, then blend in the flour. Add the stock, bring to the boil and return the meat to the pan. Cover and simmer gently for about 1½ hours.

Take out the meat and any bones. Rub the liquid through a sieve or purée in a blender. Return the purée to a clean pan. Stir in the milk and reheat but do not boil. Blend the arrowroot with the cold water, stir into the soup and heat nearly to boiling point until the soup thickens. Check the seasoning and serve.

Serves 6

Mixed vegetable soup

1 tablespoon butter
1 large onion, chopped
1 red pepper, diced
175 g carrots, diced
175 g celery, chopped
175 g swede, parsnip, or turnip, diced
550 mL chicken stock or 4 chicken cubes dissolved in 550 mL water
550 mL milk
1 bouquet garni
salt
75 g peas, frozen, or fresh shelled
3–4 teaspoons cornflour
celery leaves, snipped

Melt the butter in a large frying pan and cook the onion, pepper, carrots, and celery for 5 minutes. Stir in the swede, parsnip or turnip, stock, milk, bouquet garni and seasoning to taste.

Bring to the boil, cover and simmer gently for 25 minutes, until the vegetables are soft. Add the peas and simmer for a further 5 minutes. Remove the bouquet garni.

Blend the cornflour with a little cold water, add to the soup and simmer for 2–3 minutes, stirring. Transfer the soup to a tureen or serving bowls and sprinkle with snipped celery leaves.
Serves 6–8

Cream of mushroom soup

500 g button mushrooms
1 spring onion
4 tablespoons butter
2 tablespoons flour
1½ litres brown stock
salt and pepper
1 egg yolk
2 tablespoons thick cream
juice ½ lemon

Wipe the mushrooms and slice them finely. Peel and chop the spring onion.

Heat the butter in a large pan; when hot add the spring onion and fry quickly until golden. Add the sliced mushrooms and sauté over medium heat for about 4 minutes. Stir in the flour and cook for a further 2 minutes. Blend in the brown stock away from the heat. Return the pan to the heat, season with salt and pepper to taste and cook gently for about 10 minutes.

To thicken the soup, blend the egg yolk with the cream and lemon juice, stir into the hot soup, and reheat very gently but do not boil. Serve at once.

Serves 6–8

Cream of chicken soup

3 tablespoons butter
5 tablespoons flour
4 cups chicken stock
½ cup finely chopped cooked chicken
¼ teaspoon salt
black pepper, freshly ground
1 egg yolk
4 tablespoons thick cream

Melt the butter in a large saucepan. Stir in the flour to make a roux and cook for about 1 minute without colouring. Then draw the pan off the heat and gradually blend in the chicken stock, stirring all the time to make a smooth sauce. Return the sauce to the heat and bring to the boil.

Reduce the heat, add the cooked chicken, salt and pepper, and cook for 2 minutes.

Blend the egg yolk and cream in a bowl. Stir in a little of the hot soup, return to the pan and reheat gently, stirring constantly until thickened. Do not allow the soup to boil after the egg yolk has been added. Serve at once.

Serves 4

Cream of lettuce soup

3 heads lettuce
2 tablespoons butter
1½ teaspoons salt
freshly ground black pepper
900 mL water
150 mL thick cream
juice ½ lemon
6 small spring onions

Cut the lettuces into quarters, remove the cores and wash the leaves. Cook in boiling, salted water for 10 minutes. Drain and chop roughly.

Melt the butter in a saucepan, add the chopped lettuce, cover, then tip it a little and cook slowly for 5 minutes. Season the lettuce with salt and pepper, add the water and bring to the boil. Cover, lower the heat and simmer for 1 hour. Cool a little.

Pour the soup into a blender and blend until smooth, or rub through a sieve. Taste and adjust the seasoning.

Chill the soup very well and, just before serving, stir in the cream followed by the lemon juice.

Trim the spring onions leaving about 2.5 cm of the green part still on them. With a pair of kitchen scissors or a sharp knife, cut this green part downwards, into as many thin strips as possible. Place 1 spring onion in the centre of each bowl of soup so that the tiny strips float.

Serve very cold.
Serves 6

Chilled mushroom and lemon soup

This soup is easy to make using a blender.

450 g field mushrooms
rind 1 lemon, thinly pared
3 tablespoons lemon juice
1 clove garlic, crushed
1 teaspoon dried thyme
salt
freshly ground black pepper
900 mL chicken stock
150 mL cream
parsley, chopped for garnishing

Wash and dry the mushrooms. Reserve 1 or 2 for garnishing and slice the rest. Put them in a flat dish with the lemon rind, lemon juice, garlic, thyme and seasoning and leave them to marinate for several hours.

Place the mushrooms and the marinade in a blender with the stock and purée. Stir in the cream and adjust seasoning. Pour the soup into a serving bowl and chill. Serve garnished with the reserved mushrooms and chopped parsley.

Serves 6

Vichyssoise

Vichyssoise

900 mL chicken stock
½ teaspoon salt
4 medium potatoes
3 medium onions
3 leeks (or 1 extra onion)
½ teaspoon fresh chervil or marjoram
2 tablespoons fresh parsley
150 mL thick cream

Put the chicken stock in a large pan and bring to simmering point; add the salt. Peel the potatoes and cut into medium chunks. Peel and chop the onions. Wash, dry and slice the leeks. Add these vegetables to the stock, bring to the boil, cover, reduce heat and simmer for about 20 minutes.

Cool a little, then put the soup in a blender and blend until smooth or pass through a food mill or sieve. Chill for at least 2 hours.

Wash, dry and finely chop the chervil or marjoram and parsley. Just before serving add the herbs and cream. If you wish, put 2 or 3 overlapping raw onion rings in the centre of each soup dish before serving.

Serves 6

Fresh tomato soup

1 tablespoon butter
1 onion, thinly sliced
1 carrot, thinly sliced
1 tablespoon flour
675 g tomatoes, peeled and quartered
550 mL chicken stock
1 bay leaf
1 teaspoon sugar
pinch ground mace
salt

Melt the butter in a large pan, add the onion and carrot and sauté, covered, for 5 minutes.

Remove the pan from the heat and stir in the flour. Add the tomatoes, stock, bay leaf, sugar, mace, and seasoning to taste. Bring to the boil, cover and simmer for 20–30 minutes.

Pass the mixture through a sieve and return to the clean pan. Reheat before serving.

Serves 4–6

Hollandaise sauce
(Blender method)

4 egg yolks
salt and pepper
1 tablespoon strained lemon juice
125 g butter

Put egg yolks, salt, pepper and lemon juice into the blender bowl. Heat butter until bubbling but not coloured.

Turn blender onto low speed and very gradually pour hot butter in a thin stream onto egg yolks until sauce thickens.

Serves 6

Tartare sauce

1¼ cups mayonnaise
2 teaspoons French mustard
2 tablespoons chopped parsley
pinch of chervil and tarragon
1 tablespoon pickled cucumber, chopped
¼ cup whipped cream

Mix pickled cucumber, mustard and herbs into the mayonnaise. Stir in the whipped cream.

Use with fish fillets and garnish with shrimps, asparagus tips and lemon slices.

Béarnaise sauce
(Blender method)

¼ cup white vinegar
¼ cup tarragon vinegar
1 shallot
1 bay leaf
4 peppercorns
4 egg yolks
250 g butter
salt and pepper

Combine the vinegars with the chopped shallot, bay leaf and peppercorns in a saucepan. Bring to the boil and simmer until liquid is reduced by half. Strain, reserve liquid and cool.

Put egg yolks into blender on a low speed and very gradually add hot melted butter (no more than a teaspoon at a time).

When mixture thickens add 1 teaspoon of the vinegar mixture and a little more melted butter. Continue adding vinegar alternately with butter until both are used up and the sauce is thick and creamy.

Serves 6

Tomato sauce

2 tablespoons olive oil
2 tablespoons margarine
½ cup celery, peeled and diced
½ cup carrots, peeled and diced
¼ cup onions, peeled and diced
⅓ cup bacon trimmings and bones, unsmoked and diced
4 tablespoons flour
6 tablespoons tomato paste
1 litre white stock
1 bouquet garni
1 sprig mint
salt and pepper
pinch paprika
3 teaspoons sugar

Heat the oil and margarine in a large saucepan and fry the vegetables and bacon for 15 minutes.

Add the flour, cook for a further 5 minutes, then stir in the tomato paste and cook for 5 minutes.

Stir in the stock, add the bouquet garni and mint, bring to the boil. Simmer for 1 hour.

Season with salt, pepper, paprika and sugar, then strain through a fine conical sieve.

Serve with pasta, eggs or hamburgers, and with vegetables such as beans. This makes about 900 mL of sauce.

Variation to Tomato sauce

Portuguese sauce: To 500 mL tomato sauce, add ½ cup of skinned, seeded and chopped tomatoes and 2 chopped cloves of garlic.

Bring the sauce back to the boil for 10 minutes. Season to taste with salt and pepper.

Serve with meat, eggs and fish.

BÉCHAMEL SAUCE

1 Melt the butter in a saucepan over a low heat.

2 Draw the saucepan off the heat and add the flour to the butter to make a roux.

3 Return the saucepan to the heat and cook the roux until it bubbles, stirring constantly.

4 Remove the saucepan from the heat and blend the prepared milk into the roux, then reheat gently.

Béchamel sauce

The quantity below makes a panada or thick paste-like mixture which can be stored, covered, in a refrigerator for up to 1 week. For a thinner pouring sauce, add up to 2 cups liquid — 1¼ cups is usually sufficient; reheat gently, stirring constantly until smooth.

1 small onion, studded with 2 cloves
500 mL milk
4 tablespoons butter or margarine, or mixture of both
good ½ cup plain flour
salt and pepper
pinch nutmeg
pinch thyme

Place the onion in a saucepan with the milk. Bring gently to the boil, then remove the pan from the heat and allow to cool. Cover and leave the milk to infuse and absorb the flavour of the onion.

Melt the butter and/or margarine in a pan and stir in the flour. Cook the roux over a low heat, without letting it colour, for about 1 minute. Gradually pour in the milk, stirring continuously until a smooth sauce forms.

Add the onion and simmer the sauce for 5 minutes. Remove the onion and add salt, pepper, nutmeg and thyme. This makes 500 mL of sauce.

Variations to Béchamel sauce
Asparagus sauce: To 300 mL of prepared sauce, add 50 g cooked asparagus, blended with 1¼ cups of the water in which the asparagus was cooked.

After the sauce is cooked, remove the pan from the heat and add 4 tablespoons sour cream or natural yogurt to give the sauce a piquant flavour. Check the seasoning. This is a good sauce for chicken, veal or salmon dishes.

Mushroom sauce: Slice 150 g white button mushrooms. Boil them in the strained juice of ½ lemon and ⅝ cup stock for 3 minutes. Pour this mixture into 300 mL of béchamel sauce.

Horseradish sauce

75 g fresh horseradish root, peeled and washed
3 tablespoons wine vinegar
salt and pepper
pinch sugar
1¼ cups milk
1½ cups fresh white breadcrumbs

Grate the horseradish and soak in the wine vinegar for 1 hour. Season with salt, pepper and sugar.

Heat the milk in a saucepan and bring to the boil. Stir in the breadcrumbs and leave them to soak for 10 minutes. Blend in the horseradish mixture and serve the sauce with roast beef. This makes about 300 mL of sauce.

Note: For a change, try making horseradish sauce in the Hungarian way: mix the horseradish and vinegar mixture into 300 mL white sauce.

Spring onion butter

Flavoured butters are delicious and simple garnishes for good food.

¼ cup chopped spring onions
¼ cup red wine
15 g meat glaze
150 g butter
3 tablespoons parsley, chopped
1 tablespoon lemon juice
pinch salt
pinch pepper

Put the spring onions in a pan with the wine and boil until they are soft. Add the meat glaze and allow the mixture to cool.

Blend in the butter, parsley and lemon juice and season to taste.

Use with steaks or in sauces for grilled meat.

Herb butter

½ cup butter, softened
2 sprigs tarragon
2 sprigs parsley
1 tablespoon lemon juice or to taste
salt and pepper

Cream the butter in a bowl.

Chop tarragon and parsley finely and mix into the butter. Add the lemon juice and salt and pepper to taste.

Serve with grilled meat or fish.

Starters and snacks

THE dishes in this section are generally light and easy to prepare. The more substantial among them are suitable for snacks, family suppers or light lunches. Others are best served as appetisers. Most are versatile however and by varying quantities you can serve them on many different occasions.

Many of the recipes can be cooked ahead and frozen until wanted, reducing preparation time to simply defrosting and heating if required.

The emphasis throughout is on simple but tasty food with a dash of difference — a welcome change from those everyday standbys, soup and sandwiches.

Taramasalata

This is often served as an appetiser.

6¾ cups day-old white breadcrumbs
½ cup milk
2½ lemons
100 g cod's roe
⅝ cup olive oil
6 tablespoons thick cream
50 g black olives
good pinch paprika
salt

Put the breadcrumbs into a bowl, add the milk and mix well. Put mixture into a conical sieve and squeeze well to remove as much moisture as possible.

Cut and squeeze 1 lemon. Remove the skin from the cod's roe.

Mix the breadcrumbs and cod's roe in the bowl. Add the olive oil and lemon juice little by little, mixing with a wooden spoon. Then blend in as much of the cream as is needed to give the taramasalata the consistency of a firm mayonnaise.

Wash and dry the other lemons. Cut them into quarters.

Put the taramasalata pâté into a dish. Surround with black olives and lemon quarters and sprinkle with paprika. Serve very cold with hot toast or French bread.

Note: This may be made substituting tinned red caviar or tarama available in Greek delicatessens for the cod's roe.

Serves 8

Avocado grill

2 rashers bacon
2 long soft rolls
butter
1 large avocado
made mustard
75 g Cheddar cheese, grated

Cut the bacon into long strips and fry until crisp. Meanwhile, split, toast and butter the rolls.

Thinly slice the avocado. Reserve a few slices for decoration and arrange the rest over the toasted rolls. Smear the avocado with mustard and cover with the grated cheese.

Place under a hot grill until the cheese has melted. Top with the bacon strips and the reserved avocado slices and serve immediately.

Serves 4

Avocado grill

Cantaloup hors d'œuvre

3 small cantaloups
6 tablespoons white port
240 g Parma ham, sliced wafer-thin

Chill the cantaloups for a few hours before beginning the preparation.

Halve the fruit horizontally to make 6 cup-shaped pieces. Scoop out the seeds and drain excess juices.

With a melon baller, scoop little balls from the flesh of the melons. Replace the fruit in this form in the melon cups. Sprinkle port over each cup.

Lightly roll the thin slices of Parma ham and put them on top of the melon halves. Chill this appetiser for a short time.

Serves 6

Note: If small melons are not available use larger ones and cut the halves into 2 or 3 segments.

Artichoke hearts with cottage cheese

330 g cottage cheese
4 large globe artichokes
large bunch chives, chervil, and parsley, mixed
salt and pepper
pinch cayenne pepper
few lettuce leaves

For the blanching mixture:
juice 3 lemons
1 tablespoon flour
1.5 litres water

Put the cottage cheese in a cloth-lined sieve and leave to drain completely.

Prepare the artichoke hearts by removing the tough outer part. Rub a cut lemon over each heart to stop it blackening. Mix the juice of lemons with the flour until combined and whisk into boiling salted water. Cook the artichokes in this blanching mixture for 40 minutes or until tender. Drain and cool.

Wash the herbs; dry them well, chop, and tip them into a bowl. Add the cottage cheese, salt and pepper, cayenne pepper, and mix well with a fork.

Wash and dry the lettuce leaves. Arrange them on a serving dish. Put the artichoke hearts on the lettuce and liberally heap the cheese mixture on each one.

Serves 4

Prawn rissoles

1 medium onion
2 tablespoons oil
240 g prawns, shelled
small bunch parsley, finely chopped
3 eggs
2 tablespoons flour
1 teaspoon salt
freshly ground black pepper
shortcrust pastry made from 240 g flour
oil for deep frying

Finely chop the onion. Heat the oil in a frying pan and fry the prawns, onion, and parsley over a high heat for 4–5 minutes, stirring constantly.

Put the prawn mixture into a large bowl. Separate the egg yolks, and add to the bowl with the flour, salt, and pepper. In another bowl beat the egg whites until they form stiff peaks; gently fold them into the prawn mixture, using a spoon or spatula.

Roll out the shortcrust pastry very thinly and cut into rounds with a 10 cm diameter pastry cutter. Place a little of the prawn mixture on half of each round. Moisten the edges of the pastry with cold water and fold it over the filling. Pinch the edges together to seal.

Heat the oil in a deep saucepan: it is ready when a little flour dropped in sizzles instantly. Put in the rissoles, a few at a time, and fry for about 4 minutes or until the pastry is golden-brown.

Drain the rissoles on absorbent kitchen paper towels and serve hot.

Serves 4

PREPARING ARTICHOKE HEARTS

1 After removing the artichoke stalk and leaf tips cut around and level the base.

2 Cut away the remaining leaves to expose the artichoke heart.

3 The hairy centre of the artichoke should also be removed.

4 Using a sharp knife trim around the heart to neaten the shape.

5 Rub a cut lemon over each heart to prevent blackening. Place in cold water with added lemon juice.

6 Mix flour with lemon juice and whisk into the boiling salted water.

7 Lower the artichoke hearts into the boiling mixture and cook until tender.

8 Remove the artichoke hearts from the saucepan, drain and cool.

Tuna bread

Tuna bread

1 short loaf French bread
300 g tuna fish, canned and drained
⅜ cup mayonnaise
2 tablespoons chopped chives
juice 1 lemon
salt and pepper

Remove the breadcrumbs in the centre of the bread with a knife, leaving approximately 1.5 cm of crumb around the crust.

In a bowl, blend together the tuna, mayonnaise, chives and lemon juice. Season to taste.

Fill the hollow in the bread with this mixture and chill in the refrigerator. Serve cut into rounds on a bed of lettuce with fresh tomato segments.

Serves 4

Anchovy and garlic stuffed eggs

4 eggs
4 large cloves garlic
45 g butter
salt and pepper
8 olives
8 anchovy fillets
4 small lettuce leaves
parsley, chopped
4 small tomatoes

Put the eggs in a pan of cold water and bring to the boil. Peel the garlic cloves and add to the boiling water; remove the cloves after 7 minutes, and pound in a mortar. After the water has been boiling for 10 minutes, take out the eggs, cool them in cold water and remove their shells. Cut the shelled hard-boiled eggs in half lengthways, without damaging their surfaces and leave them to cool.

Put the butter in a bowl and work it to a very soft paste with a spoon or spatula.

Remove the yolks from the eggs, without damaging the whites. Mash and sieve the yolks and add them to the butter. Then add the garlic purée and stir well until smooth. Season with salt and pepper.

Put this paste back into the half egg whites. Decorate each with an olive with an anchovy fillet wrapped around it.

Place the lettuce leaves on a serving platter and arrange each decorated hors-d'œuvre on the lettuce leaves lengthwise. Slice the tomatoes in half horizontally and use the halves for a garnish. Sprinkle with the finely chopped parsley. Refrigerate and serve cold.

Serves 4

Anchovy and garlic stuffed eggs

Seafood hors d'œuvre

1 onion
bay leaf
bouquet garni
5 cups mussels
1 can crab, or fresh crab, cooked
1 small can tomato paste
1 tablespoon brandy
210 mL thick cream
salt
480 g prawns, fresh or frozen
small bunch parsley

Peel the onion and cut in slices.

To prepare the cooking liquid ('court bouillon'): in a large saucepan put 300 mL water, the sliced onion, bay leaf, and bouquet garni; simmer for 20 minutes.

Scrape the mussel shells to clean their surface and wash them in several changes of water. Put in the court bouillon and cook gently, stirring now and then, until they open. Discard any which do not open.

When the mussels are fully open, lift them out of the saucepan with a skimming ladle. Shell them and put in a dish.

Put the liquid through a strainer lined with a fine cloth and set it aside.

Open the can of crab, drain the crab flesh, remove any cartilage or shell, and quickly flake the flesh. Or prepare the bought crab. Wash the shell, remove the legs and break the shell to obtain the flesh. Open the centre by cracking the shell to remove the rest of the flesh.

Pour the contents of a can of tomato paste into a bowl. Stir in the brandy, then pour in the cream, stirring constantly. Then add 100 mL (5 tablespoons) of the reserved seafood liquid and mix. Add a little salt. The sauce should now be very smooth.

Divide the mussels, flaked crab and peeled prawns among six individual serving dishes and pour sauce over each serving.

Wash, dry, and chop the parsley. Sprinkle some on top of each dish.

Refrigerate and serve chilled.

Serves 6–8

Egg and anchovy mousse

This mousse is simple to make in a blender.

⅜ cup mayonnaise
8 anchovy fillets, canned and drained
salt and black pepper, freshly ground
2 tablespoons cream
1 teaspoon anchovy essence
few drops chilli sauce
4 hard-boiled eggs
1 egg white
1 sliced tomato, parsley or watercress to garnish

Put the mayonnaise in the blender with the drained anchovy fillets, seasoning, cream, anchovy essence and chilli sauce. Blend gently until smooth.

Cut the eggs into pieces and add them to the blender. Blend for a few seconds until they are finely chopped.

Whisk the egg white in a bowl until stiff and fold the contents of the blender into it. Check the seasoning and turn it into four 150 mL soufflé dishes. Cover and refrigerate for several hours. Serve garnished with sliced tomato, parsley or watercress.

Serves 4

Cheese and onion quiches

basic shortcrust pastry made with 2¼ cups flour
2 onions, chopped
2 tablespoons butter
225 g Cheddar cheese, grated
2 eggs
1¼ cups cream
salt and pepper
8 slices tomato

Preheat the oven to 220°C (425°F). Roll out the pastry on a floured board to a thickness of 3 mm and use it to line eight 9 cm individual flan tins. Bake blind for 15 minutes.

Fry the onion in the butter until transparent and then divide it, with the cheese, between the flan cases. Whip eggs, cream and seasoning, and pour into the cases. Place a slice of tomato on top of each quiche, and bake for 30 minutes.

They can be eaten immediately, hot or cold. To freeze, leave to cool and wrap each quiche separately in foil or polythene. Seal and label before placing them in the freezer.

To serve, thaw the quiches for 12 hours in the refrigerator. If you wish to reheat them, place them in the oven, preheated to 190°C (375°F), for 10–12 minutes.

Chinese sausage pancakes

1¾ cups basic pancake batter
350 g bean sprouts
4 sausages, cooked and chopped
1 tablespoon soya sauce
2 tablespoons mango chutney
oil for deep frying

Sauce:
225 g peeled tomatoes, canned or fresh
1 tablespoon tomato paste
¼ cup vinegar
3 tablespoons brown sugar
1 carrot, grated
2 gherkins, finely chopped
rind ½ orange, grated

Reserve ½ cup of the pancake batter and use the rest to make 8 pancakes. In a bowl, mix the bean sprouts, chopped sausage, soya sauce and chutney. Divide the mixture between the 8 pancakes and roll each one up, sealing the edges with a little of the reserved batter.

Heat the oil for deep frying to 190°C (375°F). Dip each pancake in the remaining batter so that they are very lightly coated, and fry them in the oil until they are crisp and golden-brown. Drain on absorbent paper.

If you wish to eat them immediately, place all the sauce ingredients in a saucepan and mix well. Simmer over a gentle heat for 8 minutes. Place the pancakes on a serving dish and cover with sauce.

To freeze: cool the pancakes before wrapping them individually in aluminium foil. Place them in a container and label them before placing them in the freezer. Pour the prepared sauce into a freezing container. Seal, label and place it in the freezer.

To serve: thaw the sauce overnight in the refrigerator. Place it in a saucepan and gently reheat. Unwrap the pancakes and fry them in oil just long enough to thaw and reheat them. Place the reheated pancakes on a serving dish and cover with the sauce.

Serves 4

Chinese sausage pancakes

Brandy and orange pancakes

1 quantity basic pancake batter
finely grated rind 1 orange
¼ cup sugar
¼ cup butter
juice 2 oranges
6 tablespoons brandy

Make up the pancake batter, adding the grated orange rind with the egg, and make the pancakes following instructions for the Basic Pancake recipe (see 'Desserts' chapter). Fold the pancakes in quarters.

Gently heat the sugar in a frying pan, shaking the pan until the sugar is golden-brown. Remove from the heat and add the butter, orange juice and half the brandy.

Place the folded pancakes in the pan and simmer for a few minutes, spooning the sauce over.

Warm the remaining brandy, pour it over the pancakes, light and serve immediately.

Serves 4

Brandy and orange pancakes

Deep-fried chicken balls

This is a good way to use up leftover chicken, and the dish can be frozen if wanted.

675 g chicken, cooked and minced
¼ cup minced pork fat
4 water chestnuts, minced
1 spring onion, minced
1 thin slice fresh root ginger, minced
1 egg
1 tablespoon cornflour
½ teaspoon salt
1 tablespoon sherry
oil for deep frying
⅝ cup coating batter

In a bowl, mix the chicken, fat, water chestnuts, spring onion, ginger, egg, cornflour, salt and sherry until smooth. Form the mixture into balls, 4 cm in diameter.

Heat the oil for deep frying. Dip the chicken balls, a few at a time, in the batter and fry them in the oil until light golden-brown, drain and leave to cool. If freezing, place in a container, seal, label and freeze. To serve, re-fry the chicken balls in oil, heated for deep frying, until dark golden-brown. Drain and serve.

Serves 4

Fish and shellfish

THE quality of fish depends largely on its freshness so great care should be taken when buying. Check that the skin is shiny and bright and the scales do not cling tightly. The gills should be a clear bright red, free from shine.

The eyes should be bright, clear, and full (not faded, cloudy, or sunken). The flesh should be firm and elastic to the touch and should not separate easily from the bone. Above all, the fish should not smell strongly or unpleasantly — it should have only a mild, characteristic odour. Given the wide variety and excellent quality of Australian seafood it should always be possible to choose good, fresh produce.

The cardinal rule in fish cookery is that only a minimum of cooking is required; the tender flesh will disintegrate and the delicate flavour will be lost if a dish is overcooked.

Seafood garnishes

Creamed mussels: Stir 100g mussels into 1½ cups velouté sauce. Heap a spoonful onto each fillet.

Tartare sauce: Mix 1¼ cups mayonnaise with 2 teaspoons French mustard, 2 tablespoons chopped parsley, a pinch of chervil and tarragon and 1 tablespoon chopped, pickled cucumber. Stir in ¼ cup whipped cream. Place a spoonful on each fillet and garnish with prawns, asparagus tips and lemon slices.

Caviar and tomato: Place a thin slice of lemon, a slice of tomato and a spoonful of black caviar onto each fillet.

Sauce hollandaise: Pour a generous pat of hollandaise sauce (see 'Soups, sauces and garnishes' chapter) onto each fried fish fillet and garnish with onion rings and chopped chives.

Prawns in hot sauce: Fry 1 chopped onion in 4 tablespoons butter and oil. Add a few chopped capers and 3 tablespoons brandy. Stir in ¼ cup tomato paste, 2 drops tabasco sauce and 100 mL cream. Season, add 225 g peeled prawns and boil for 5 minutes. Heap a spoonful of sauce onto fried fish fillets and garnish with peeled prawns.

Seafood garnishes (clockwise from the top): Creamed mussels, tartare sauce, sauce hollandaise, prawns in hot sauce, caviar and tomato

Barramundi provençale (See page 30)

Barramundi provençale

3 medium onions, chopped
3 cloves garlic, crushed
¼ cup olive oil
2 tablespoons butter
2 large tins tomatoes
1 teaspoon dried rosemary
1 bay leaf
pinch ground fennel
2 cups red wine
180 mL tomato paste
½ cup pine nuts
¼ cup capers
¼ cup black olives, chopped
salt and pepper
750 g barramundi (or cod) fillets
1 tablespoon seasoned flour
parsley, chopped

Fry onions and garlic in oil and butter. Add tomatoes, rosemary, bay leaf and fennel. Blend in wine and tomato paste. Cook gently until thickened. Add nuts, capers, olives and season. Cook for 30 minutes.

Dredge fillets with seasoned flour. Fry in hot oil until golden-brown on both sides. Pour sauce over fish and sprinkle with chopped parsley.

Serves 4

Shallow-fried John Dory

1 kg John Dory fillets
salt and pepper
1 cup flour
1 egg, beaten
150 mL oil
4 cups fresh white breadcrumbs
3 tablespoons butter
2 lemons
parsley, chopped

Wash and dry the fillets, remove the skin and sprinkle with salt and pepper. Coat the fillets in flour.

Blend the beaten egg with 1 tablespoon oil. Dip the fillets into this mixture and coat with the breadcrumbs. Decorate the fillets by making a criss-cross pattern on both sides with a knife.

Heat the butter and remaining oil in a frying pan. Add the fish and fry gently for 2–3 minutes on each side until lightly browned. Drain on absorbent paper.

Arrange the fish on a warmed serving dish and decorate with lemon halves and slices. Serve with parsley butter.

Serves 4

Note: Bream, red mullet or cod can be substituted for John Dory in this recipe.

Trout meunière

4 trout (about 225 g each)
salt and pepper
½ cup flour
7–8 tablespoons butter
2 tablespoons oil
2 lemons
1 tablespoon chopped parsley

Wash and dry the trout, season with salt and pepper then roll them in flour and shake off the excess.

Heat 4 tablespoons butter and the oil in a large, oval frying pan. When foaming, add the trout and cook gently on both sides.

Meanwhile, cannelle a lemon and slice thinly. Peel another lemon and cut into slices.

Arrange the cooked trout on a buttered serving dish and sprinkle with the chopped parsley. Keep hot.

Heat the remainder of the butter in a pan until it is frothing and pour over the trout. Garnish with the lemon slices.

Serves 4

TROUT MEUNIÈRE

1. After dredging in flour place the trout in foaming butter and oil mixture in a pan.

2. Turn carefully to cook the other side.

3. Prepare a serving dish for the trout and arrange them decoratively.

4. Heat the remaining butter mixture until it is frothing. Pour over the trout.

Note: Sole or flounder can be used instead of trout. Use the fish whole and do not remove the white skin or take off the fillets before serving.

Variations to Trout meunière

Belle meunière: Garnish the trout with peeled, seeded tomatoes and sautéed mushrooms.
Bretonne: Garnish with peeled prawns and sliced sautéed mushrooms.
Doria: Decorate with chopped, sautéed cucumber.
Marseillaise: Garnish with sautéed eggplant, tomatoes and garlic butter.

Trout meunière

Leatherjacket with green anchovy butter

4 large leatherjacket fillets
salt and pepper
juice of ½ lemon

Green anchovy butter:
½ bunch watercress
2 tablespoons butter
4 anchovy fillets
black pepper, freshly ground

Drop watercress into a pan of boiling water. As soon as it boils remove from heat and drain. Put cress through a sieve with anchovies, or blend them in a food processor.

Soften butter slightly, gradually beat in cress purée, and add pepper. Divide into eight small portions and chill until firm.

Sprinkle fish fillets with lemon juice and seasoning. Grill on both sides, turning once. Serve each fillet topped with two portions butter.
Serves 4

Silver bream with basil

1 whole silver bream (about 1 kg)
2 cloves garlic, slivered
1 large onion, chopped
4 tablespoons oil
1 can tomatoes
1 teaspoon sugar
1 tablespoon chopped parsley
1 tablespoon chopped fresh basil, or ¼ teaspoon dried basil
salt and pepper
½ cup white wine
125 g button mushrooms
¼ cup melted butter

Make incisions into fish and insert garlic. Fry onion in half the oil until softened. Add chopped tomatoes and their juice, sugar and herbs and season. Cook gently for five minutes.

Spoon half the mixture into an ovenproof dish and lay the fish on top. Pour over the remaining sauce mixture and the wine.

Cover and bake in a moderate oven 40 minutes or until fish flakes easily.

Lightly sauté mushrooms in butter, spoon over fish and return to the oven for 5 minutes.

Serve with French-fried potatoes and tossed salad.
Serves 4

Snapper mexicana

1 whole snapper (about 2 kg)
lemon juice
2 onions, chopped
¼ cup olive oil
2 teaspoons Mexican-style chilli powder
¼ teaspoon tabasco sauce
salt and pepper
1¼ cups dry red wine
1¼ cups chicken stock
½ cup blanched, slivered almonds
2 tablespoons butter

Brush fish with lemon juice, inside and out, and place in a greased baking dish.

Fry onion in oil until softened. Stir in chilli powder and tabasco sauce and season. Spread mixture over fish. Add the red wine and chicken stock.

Bake, covered, in a moderate oven, for 20 minutes or until fish flakes easily, basting once or twice with pan juices.

Mix almonds with butter and sprinkle over fish. Place under heated griller for a few minutes to brown almonds. Serve the snapper with boiled rice and tossed salad.
Serves 6

Silver bream with basil

Oysters Rockefeller

Oysters can be served raw in their shells, or they can be grilled and served in a creamy sauce. Always choose oyster shells which are tightly shut. Scrub and wash the shells and open by inserting a special oyster knife into the hinge of the shell to cut through the muscles.

---

24 oysters
2 (375 g) packages frozen chopped spinach, or fresh spinach, cooked and thoroughly drained
12 spring onions, finely chopped
6 tablespoons finely chopped parsley
½ cup fine dry breadcrumbs
½ teaspoon salt
black pepper, freshly ground
⅛ teaspoon cayenne pepper
½ cup melted butter

It is easier to have the fishmonger open the oysters for you. Loosen each oyster from the shell and remove. Scrub the shells and dry thoroughly. Return the oysters to their shells and arrange them in a baking dish lined with rock salt.

Combine all the remaining ingredients in a mixing bowl. Spread a spoonful of the mixture over each oyster.

Bake in a 230°C (450°F), oven for no longer than 10 minutes. Transfer to individual plates and serve immediately.

Serves 4

Lobster gratiné

Though generally expensive, crabs and lobsters are truly a delicacy and well worth preparing for a special dinner. A lobster has firm, white meat throughout the body as well as soft parts which are also delicious. A crab contains both brown and white edible meat. The claws of both crabs and lobsters contain the most delicate meat, tinged with pink.

---

2 lobsters, about 1 kg each
¼ cup mayonnaise
¼ cup thick cream
½ teaspoon paprika
few drops anchovy essence
½ cup cheese, grated
1 tablespoon sherry
1 teaspoon made mustard
salt and pepper
1 egg yolk

Plunge the lobsters into a large pot of boiling water and cook for 10 minutes or until they are bright pink.

Remove from the water and allow to cool. With a sharp knife split the lobsters down the length of the body.

Take out the meat and dice. Blend together the mayonnaise, cream, paprika and anchovy essence and mix the lobster meat into it. Divide the mixture between the shell halves.

Over low heat, melt the cheese with the sherry and mustard, season and remove from the heat. Beat in the egg yolk. Cover the lobster halves evenly with a thick layer of the cheese sauce. Place under a hot grill until the cheese is golden-brown.

Serves 4

Lobster gratiné

Prawns with bean sprouts

225 g firm white fish, skinned, boned and cut into strips
½ cup flour
salt and pepper
¼ cup oil
1 onion, chopped
100 g button mushrooms, quartered
1 clove garlic, crushed
1¼ cups small prawns, cooked and peeled
675 g bean sprouts
1 teaspoon soya sauce
1 small lettuce, shredded

Roll the fish in flour seasoned with salt and pepper. Shake off excess.

Heat the oil in a large frying pan or wok. Quickly fry the onion for 2 minutes. Add the mushrooms, garlic and fish. Toss and cook gently for 4 minutes, stirring continuously. Add the prawns, half of the bean sprouts and seasoning. Toss well and cook for 4 more minutes.

Add the soya sauce. Remove the frying pan or wok from the stove and add the shredded lettuce. Toss. Transfer this mixture to a warm serving dish and keep warm. Toss the remaining bean sprouts in the pan for a few minutes and place them in a serving bowl.

Serve the prawn dish accompanied by the bean sprouts.

Serves 4

Note: This is a Chinese style recipe involving very quick but intense cooking. You can use any cooked shellfish, for example, mussels, or scallops. Add cooked Chinese noodles for a more substantial dish or replace the lettuce with shredded red and green peppers.

Moules marinières

Fresh mussels *must* be alive when you buy them. Wash several times in clean water to remove any sand or grit and discard any with broken or gaping shells. Never overcook mussels but steam them gently. When they are cooked the shells will open wide.

48 mussels in their shells
3 tablespoons butter
1 onion, finely chopped
1¼ cups dry white wine
2 sprigs thyme
1 bay leaf
salt and pepper
2 teaspoons flour
1 tablespoon chopped parsley

Clean, scrape and rinse the mussels. Melt 2 tablespoons butter in a saucepan and sauté the onion until soft.

Add the wine, herbs and seasoning. Simmer for 10 minutes, then add the mussels. Cover the pan and bring to the boil. Cook the mussels for about 3–5 minutes, shaking the pan occasionally.

Remove the mussels and keep warm. Mix the remaining butter with the flour. Boil the liquid to reduce by half, then thicken with the butter and flour mixture. Pour the sauce over the mussels and sprinkle with parsley.

Serves 4

Meat

MEAT, although sometimes expensive, is still the major part of everyday meals and there is a wide choice available. The texture and flavour of cheaper cuts can be improved if they are marinated for several hours. Wine, beer or cider or an acidic mixture of fruit juices and vinegar all have a tenderising effect as well as adding flavour.

Beef should always be seasoned before cooking. Use salt and freshly ground black pepper and for additional flavour use herbs or spices as well. Try inserting a clove of garlic or a small piece of onion into the meat itself.

Lamb is easy to cook and has a distinctive flavour and abundant natural fat which means that most cuts are tender. In England, the United States and Australia, most people prefer their lamb well cooked but in Europe it is usually eaten slightly underdone and still pink in the centre.

Herbs go very well with lamb and it is well worth experimenting with different combinations in roasts and casseroles. As lamb has a rather delicate flavour of its own take care not to overdo the use of herbs but thyme, oregano, marjoram, basil, rosemary, parsley and mint should all enhance its flavour.

Veal is a tender meat, also with a delicate flavour so care should be taken not to swamp its natural taste with very rich sauces or by over-seasoning.

As a rule pork requires longer, slower cooking than beef, lamb or veal. However it should be moist and tender when served, so avoid the danger of letting it dry out and lose flavour by over-zealous regard for the rule.

Tips for cooking roast beef

If you follow the basic rules for roasting you should always have good results. Season the joint lightly with salt and freshly ground pepper and handle the meat very gently; never pierce it with a knife or skewer. It is important that the meat juices should stay intact.

Rub the meat well with oil or fat — a mixture of butter and lard works well. Use 25 g for every 450 g meat. Baste the meat frequently during cooking.

If you can, stand the joint on a rack, above a roasting pan to catch the juices. Alternatively, place the joint on a bed of root vegetables (carrots, celery, and onions) or meat bones. The vegetable and meat juices can be used as a base for the gravy.

Use a meat thermometer if you like meat well-done. It is essential if you are to obtain good results. Insert it into the meat but take care that it does not touch the bone.

Preheat the oven to 220°C (425°F). Cook the meat on the middle shelf and sear it at the high temperature. Then, if you like beef underdone, continue cooking at this temperature. If you prefer well-done beef, lower the temperature to 190°C (275°F).

Roast beef is traditionally served with roast potatoes, Yorkshire pudding and horseradish sauce (see 'Soups, sauces and garnishes' chapter) and mustard. Rest the joint for 15 minutes before carving.

Yorkshire pudding

2 eggs
1¼ cups flour, sifted
1¼ cups water, or milk and water mixed
pinch salt

Beat the eggs well then stir in the flour. Add the liquid and beat for 3 to 4 minutes to obtain a smooth batter. Season with the salt and leave the batter to rest for 1 hour.

If the oven is not already hot, preheat it to 190°C (375°F).

Place a teaspoon of the meat fat and juices in the bottom of each patty tin (use a muffin pan) and heat in the oven for 5 minutes. Then half-fill them with batter and bake for 15–20 minutes until well-risen and golden.

Roast beef

Osso buco (See page 47)

Burgundy beef

This is a classic, rich, delicious stew — a fine way of cooking tougher cuts of beef.

The cooking liquor of stews and casseroles should be slightly acid, to help tenderise the meat. Wine, cider, beer, tomato paste or fruit juices can be used.

½ cup oil
1 kg silverside, cut into 2.5 cm cubes
1 carrot, thinly sliced
1 large onion, thinly sliced
4 tablespoons flour
2½ cups dry red wine
salt and pepper
2 cloves garlic, peeled and crushed
1 bouquet garni
100 g small onions, peeled
1 tablespoon sugar
¼ cup butter
100 g streaky bacon rashers, cut in strips
100 g mushrooms, chopped or whole

Heat three-quarters of the oil in a large, heavy-based saucepan, put the pieces of beef into it and brown over a high heat. Remove the meat, then pour out any remaining oil and add the slices of carrot and onion. Let them brown lightly, then add the flour and cook, stirring constantly with a wooden spoon.

Mix in all the wine. Bring to the boil and allow at least a third of it to evaporate on a high heat. Return the meat to the pan and add enough cold water to cover it. Add salt, pepper, garlic and the bouquet garni. Cover and cook gently for 2½ hours.

Put the small onions in a pan with the sugar, butter and enough water to cover. Cover and cook until the water has evaporated. When a golden caramel mixture remains, roll the small onions in it and put to one side.

Heat the rest of the oil in a pan and lightly fry the bacon. Drain and reserve. Fry the mushrooms in the same oil and reserve.

When the stew is cooked, sieve the sauce and return it to the pan. Add the small onions, bacon and mushrooms and cook for a further 10 minutes.

Serves 6–8

Sirloin with peppercorns and garlic

Sirloin with peppercorns and garlic

4 × 350 g sirloin steaks, 2.5 cm thick
12 black peppercorns
4 cloves garlic, thinly sliced
⅓ cup oil
salt

Trim the fat from the steaks. Crush the peppercorns and sprinkle over both sides of the steaks, pressing well into the meat.

Make several slits in the surface of the steaks and insert the slices of garlic into the slits. Brush the steaks with oil and then cook them under a grill, over a charcoal fire, or in a heavy-based frying pan. Cook for 2 minutes on both sides for underdone meat, 4 minutes for medium or 8 minutes for well-done.

Serves 4

Beef goulash

675 g stewing beef, cut in 3 cm cubes
⅜ cup oil
3 medium onions, thinly sliced
1 tablespoon paprika
good pinch cumin
2 cloves garlic, crushed
salt and pepper
pinch marjoram
3 tomatoes, skinned, seeded and chopped
1 green pepper, shredded
⅝ cup red wine
1 beef stock
675 g potatoes, peeled
3 tablespoons cornflour
⅝ cup sour cream

Heat the oil in a pan and fry the onion for 4 minutes until pale brown. Add the meat, reduce the heat and cook gently for 8 minutes, stirring from time to time.

Add the paprika, cumin, garlic, seasoning and marjoram and cook for 1 minute more. Add the tomatoes and pepper and simmer for another 10 minutes. Stir in the wine and stock. Cook gently for 1½ hours.

Towards the end of the cooking time, boil the potatoes in salted water for 18 minutes.

When ready to serve, dissolve the cornflour in ⅝ cup water, stir into the meat and cook for 2–3 minutes until thickened.

Serve the goulash with the sour cream and boiled potatoes.
Serves 6

Note: Shell pasta and rice can be served with this dish instead of boiled potatoes, if preferred.

Beef and eggplant pie

This pie can be made ahead and stored in the freezer.

2 eggplants, sliced
salt and pepper
⅝ cup butter
2 onions, peeled and chopped
450 g minced beef
⅞ cup beef stock
4 tablespoons flour
225 g frozen puff pastry, thawed
225 g tomatoes, sliced
1 tablespoon chopped parsley
½ teaspoon oregano
milk to glaze

Sprinkle the eggplant slices with salt and leave to drain in a colander for 30 minutes. Rinse and dry.

Preheat the oven to 190°C (375°F).

Melt ½ cup of the butter in a frying pan and fry the eggplants on both sides until golden-brown. Drain. Melt the remaining butter and fry the onion and minced beef gently for 15 minutes. Add the stock and seasoning and simmer gently for a further 15 minutes.

Blend the flour with a little water, add it to the beef and simmer for 2 minutes, stirring.

Roll out two-thirds of the pastry and use to line the base and sides of a 450 g aluminium foil loaf tin. Cover the base of the dish with half the eggplant slices. Spoon over half the beef and top with half the tomato slices. Sprinkle the herbs over the tomato. Cover with remaining eggplant slices, beef and tomato slices.

Roll out the remaining pastry to form a 'lid'. Dampen the edge of the pastry base, cover with the 'lid' and press the edges together. Trim and flute with the back of a knife. Decorate with leaves made from the pastry trimmings and brush with milk.

Bake for 50 minutes. Serve the pie immediately or allow it to cool, wrap with aluminium foil, seal, label and freeze.

Allow the frozen pie to thaw completely, then reheat in an oven preheated to 180°C (350°F), for 30–35 minutes.
Serves 6

Pasta shepherds pie

This dish can also be cooked ahead and frozen until wanted.

2 tablespoons oil
1 onion, peeled and sliced
450 g minced beef
1 clove garlic, crushed
400 g canned tomatoes
1 tablespoon tomato paste
1 teaspoon mixed herbs
salt and pepper
2 cups macaroni
2 eggs
300 mL sour cream or natural yogurt
¾ cup grated cheese

Preheat the oven to 190°C (375°F).
Heat the oil in a large pan and fry the onion until soft but not golden. Add the beef and fry until browned.
Add the garlic, canned tomatoes and juice, tomato paste, herbs and seasoning. Bring to the boil and simmer for 20 minutes.
Meanwhile, cook the pasta in boiling salted water for 8–10 minutes until just tender. Drain.
Beat the eggs and mix with the sour cream or yogurt. Add two-thirds of the cheese and the pasta.
Transfer the meat mixture to an ovenproof dish and pour the pasta mixture over the top. Sprinkle with the remaining cheese and bake for 25–30 minutes.
Serve immediately or allow to cool, wrap and freeze. Reheat from frozen in an oven pre-heated to 180°C (350°F) for 40–50 minutes.
Serves 6

Steak and kidney pie

2 tablespoons oil
450 g lean chuck steak, cubed
225 g calves kidneys (or lambs or ox), trimmed and quartered
1 onion, chopped
4 tablespoons flour
salt and pepper
1½ cups beef stock
1 bouquet garni
¾ cup broad beans, canned or frozen and thawed
450 g flaky pastry
1 egg, beaten

Heat the oil in a large pan and sauté the pieces of steak and kidney for 5 minutes until lightly brown. Lower the heat and add the onion. Cook gently for 5 minutes. Stir in the flour and cook for a few minutes more. Season.
Pour over the stock. Add bouquet garni and bring to the boil. Turn the heat down, cover and simmer for 1½ hours or until the meat is tender.
Add the broad beans and transfer to a medium-sized pie dish.
Preheat the oven to 220°C (425°F).
Roll out the flaky pastry on a floured surface until it is 5 cm wider all round than the dish. Prick all over with a fork. Cut out a 2.5 cm strip of pastry and place on the rim of the dish. Brush with water. Then place the pastry lid on top. Press edges together. Cut the pastry trimmings into leaf shapes and decorate the pie with them. Brush with the beaten egg. Leave in a cool place for 20 minutes.
Bake for 30 minutes. Serve hot.
Serves 4

Stuffed leg of lamb

2 tablespoons currants
6 tablespoons butter
1 onion, chopped
4 apples, peeled, cored, and diced
¾ cup long-grain rice
salt and pepper
2 kg leg of lamb, boned
½ cup oil
½ cup stock
juice 1 lemon

Preheat the oven to 200°C (400°F).
Soak the currants in water. Heat the butter in a frying pan. Fry the onion gently, add the apples and cook until all the liquid evaporates.
Boil the rice for 10 minutes.
Mix the onion and apples with the drained currants and rice. Season with salt and pepper. Stuff the leg with the mixture and sew up the opening. Season and brush with oil.
Roast for 2¼ hours in all, 35 minutes at 200°C (400°F), and 1 hour 40 minutes with the temperature reduced to 180°C (350°F).
When the leg is cooked, remove from the pan and put on a serving dish. Make a gravy with the pan juices and stock and flavour with lemon juice.
Serves 6–8

Shoulder of lamb with apricot and pawpaw sauce

1 kg shoulder of young lamb
salt and pepper
4 tablespoons butter
1 teaspoon mixed spice
2 tablespoons honey
1 pawpaw
1 cup canned apricots
few sprigs parsley for decoration

Preheat the oven to 200°C (400°F).
Season the lamb with salt and pepper, cover with the butter and place in a roasting tin.
Roast the meat for ½ hour, then reduce the temperature to 180°C (350°F) for a further ½ hour.
Combine the mixed spice with the honey and baste the meat with this during roasting.
Scoop out the pawpaw into balls with a melon baller. Add the canned apricots and pawpaw to the pan ¼ hour before the end of roasting.
When cooked, remove the meat and place on a dish. Surround it with the apricots and pawpaw.
Use some of the canned juice to loosen the browned sediment in the tin. Boil, season, strain and serve separately.
Garnish the dish with sprigs of parsley and serve with new potatoes and peas.
Serves 4

Chinese spare ribs

1.5 kg breast of lamb
1 L boiling water
2 tablespoons vinegar

Sauce:
2 tablespoons soya sauce
2 tablespoons clear honey
2 tablespoons plum jam
1 tablespoon white vinegar
1 teaspoon Worcestershire sauce
1 teaspoon dry mustard
1 teaspoon tomato paste
juice ½ lemon

Remove the thin skin and any excess fat from the breast. Cut between each bone.
Place the meat in the boiling water and vinegar and simmer for ¼ hour.
Preheat the oven to 180°C (350°F).
Mix all the sauce ingredients together, and heat.
Drain the lamb, place in a roasting tin. Pour the sauce over.
Bake for ½ hour, basting frequently. Increase the heat to 200°C (400°F) and cook for a further 20 minutes.
Serves 6–8

Lamb Louise

This is another dish suitable for freezing.

8 lamb loin chops
2 tablespoons oil
8 spring onions or 3 medium onions, chopped
2 tablespoons flour
1¼ cups apple juice
2 tablespoons soya sauce
1 teaspoon sugar
1 tablespoon chopped mint
2 red apples
2 tablespoons butter
1 tablespoon chopped parsley

Brown the chops lightly on both sides in the oil. Drain and remove them from the pan, and keep warm. Add the onions to the pan and cook until lightly browned.
Stir in the flour and cook for 1 minutes. Add the apple juice and bring to the boil, stirring.
Lower the heat to a simmer; add the soya sauce, sugar and mint. Return the chops to the pan, cover and simmer for 30 minutes.
To freeze, place the chops and sauce in a container, seal and label. Thaw for 12 hours in a refrigerator, place in a pan and reheat slowly over low heat before serving.
To serve, core and slice the apples and cook gently in the butter for 5–10 minutes. Mix the sliced apples into the sauce, place on a serving dish, sprinkle with parsley and serve.
Serves 4
Note: Do not cook the apples in advance if the dish is to be frozen: prepare them just before serving.

Shoulder of lamb with apricot and pawpaw sauce

Norfolk parcel

Breast of lamb is one of the cheapest cuts but carefully cooked, it provides a fine, tasty meal.

The butcher will bone it for you and it is delicious served rolled and roasted or in a parcel like this.

1 kg boned breast of lamb, cut in 4 equal pieces
2 tablespoons oil
2 tablespoons butter

Stuffing:
2 large onions, chopped
2 tablespoons fat,
⅝ cup chicken stock
225 g sausage-meat
2 cups fresh breadcrumbs
salt and pepper
1 tablespoon fresh sage, finely chopped
1 tablespoon chutney

Trim any excess fat from the meat and beat it lightly with a rolling pin or meat mallet. Preheat the oven to 200°C (400°F).

To make the stuffing, fry the onion gently in the fat until soft but not browned. Add the stock and boil for 5 minutes until the liquid is well reduced. Remove from the heat and stir in the sausage-meat, breadcrumbs, a pinch of salt and pepper, sage and chutney. Blend well to make a thick paste.

Divide the stuffing into 4 and spread it over the pieces of meat. Place the pieces of meat on top of each other to make a sandwich, and tie them together neatly with fine string. Season with salt and pepper and brush the oil and butter over the top and sides.

Roast the meat parcel in the oven for 20 minutes. Then turn the oven temperature down to 180°C (350°F) for 1½–2 hours, basting the meat frequently. Place the meat on a heated serving dish. Strain fat from the cooking juices and pour the rest over the meat.

Serves 6–8

Norfolk parcel

Veal

Notes on cooking veal

Veal is an expensive meat containing little fat. Escalopes, one of the choicest cuts, come from the leg of the calf. They contain no fat or gristle, are cut about 5 mm thick and are then usually beaten with a mallet or rolling pin until very thin. Scaloppines are similar, but are cut against the grain of the meat rather than with it. Veal has a very light flavour and for this reason is often served with interesting sauces. Pot roasting on a bed of vegetables, or braising, are tastier ways to cook veal than a simple roast.

Osso buco with artichoke hearts

2 tablespoons flour
salt and pepper
8 slices knuckle of veal, 2.5 cm thick
2 tablespoons butter
1 large onion, sliced
2 cloves garlic, peeled and crushed
2 carrots, sliced
2 sticks celery, finely chopped
¾ cup dry white wine
4 large tomatoes, skinned, seeded and chopped
1 tablespoon tomato paste
1 bay leaf
pinch dried rosemary
8 canned artichoke hearts (optional)
juice and grated peel 1 lemon
1 tablespoon chopped parsley

Season the flour with salt and pepper. Dredge the veal in it. Heat the butter in a frying pan and brown the veal. Take out and place in a heavy-bottomed pan.

Lightly fry the onion, garlic, carrots and celery in the oil, then add to the meat.

Pour the wine over the meat and vegetables. Bring to the boil then lower heat to simmering. Stir in the tomatoes, tomato paste, bay leaf and rosemary. Season to taste. Cover and leave to simmer for 1 hour or until the meat is tender.

Add the drained artichoke hearts and the juice and grated rind of the lemon. Cook for 10 minutes more. Immediately before serving sprinkle on the chopped parsley. Serve with plain boiled potatoes, rice or noodles and a crisp green salad.

Serves 4

Note: This dish can also be made using veal knuckles 5 cm thick. Allow one per portion and cook for 1½ hours.

The marrow inside the knuckle is delicious: eat it with the stew.

Braised veal in mushroom sauce

1.2 kg boned and rolled veal joint (leg or shoulder)
6 tablespoons butter
2 spring onions, chopped
2 onions, chopped
1 sprig thyme
1 bay leaf
salt and pepper
400 mL cider
225 g mushrooms, chopped
1 egg yolk
½ cup cream
2 tablespoons chopped parsley

Fry the veal gently in ¼ cup of the butter until browned on all sides. Lift out. Fry the spring onions and onions in the same fat until softened.

Return the veal to the pan and add the thyme, bay leaf, salt and pepper to taste and the cider. Bring to the boil, cover and cook over a low heat for 1½ hours.

Fry the mushrooms in the rest of the butter for 3–4 minutes.

When the veal has cooked for 1½ hours add the mushrooms to the pan and continue cooking for a further 10 minutes.

Drain the veal and place on a serving dish. Keep warm. Discard the thyme and bay leaf.

Beat the egg yolk with the cream. Beat into the cooking liquid and cook gently until thickened. Cover the meat with this sauce, sprinkle with the parsley and serve hot.

Serves 6

Veal escalopes in Marsala

4 veal escalopes
4 tablespoons butter
½ cup Marsala
¾ cup gravy or thickened stock
pinch cayenne pepper

Place the veal escalopes between 2 sheets of dampened greaseproof paper and beat with a mallet or rolling pin until they are 3 mm thick.

Heat the butter in a frying pan and fry the escalopes until well browned. Transfer them to a warmed serving dish and keep hot.

Add the Marsala to the fat in the pan and boil for 5 minutes, stirring well. Add the gravy or stock and cayenne, mix well and pour the sauce over the veal.

Serves 4

Crown roast of pork

Pork is available in a variety of cuts and can be roasted, grilled, fried, casseroled, cured, boiled or made into sausages.

Pork is traditionally served with apple or gooseberry sauce but spices such as cloves and paprika go well with it too in either a marinade or a tart apple sauce. Herbs such as thyme, sage, rosemary and garlic all enhance its flavour. In oriental dishes it is often served with ginger, soya sauce or pineapple.

---

2 loins of pork, each containing 8 chops, chined
4 tablespoons melted butter
1 onion, finely chopped
2 sticks celery, finely chopped
225 g pork sausage-meat
2 cups fresh breadcrumbs
1 teaspoon rosemary
2 tablespoons finely chopped parsley
½ teaspoon thyme
salt and pepper
¼ cup chicken stock

Remove the chine bone from the loins. Cut 4 cm of the fat away from the ends of the bones. Trim away the sinew from between the bones.

Bend the 2 loins round to form the crown and secure with string. Place the crown in a roasting pan and brush all over the outside with the melted butter. Wrap pieces of aluminium foil round the ends of the bones to prevent them burning.

Preheat the oven to 180°C (350°F). Prepare the stuffing: heat the remaining butter in a frying pan, add the onion and celery and fry until soft.

Add the sausage-meat and cook until all the fat has run out of the meat. Drain the excess fat from the pan.

Stir in the breadcrumbs, rosemary, parsley, thyme, seasoning and stock and mix.

Place the stuffing in the centre of the crown and cover the stuffing with a circle of foil.

Roast the crown in the oven, allowing 30 minutes per 450 g of meat.

Before serving, remove the pieces of foil and place a cutlet frill on the end of each bone. Serve the roast garnished with peas and roast potatoes.

Serves 8

Crown roast of pork served with peas and roast potatoes

CROWN ROAST PORK

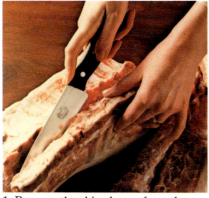
1 Remove the chine bones from the two pork joints.

2 Cut 4 cm of fat away from the ends of the bones.

3 Trim away the sinew from between the bones.

4 Bend the two joints around to form the crown and secure with string.

5 Place the crown in a roasting dish and brush with melted butter.

6 Wrap aluminium foil around the ends of the bones.

7 Fry the onion and celery in the butter until they are soft.

8 Add the sausagemeat and cook until fat runs out of the meat.

9 Drain this excess fat from the pan.

10 Add the breadcrumbs, rosemary, parsley, seasoning and stock.

11 Place the stuffing mixture in the centre of the crown.

12 Cover the stuffing with a circle of aluminium foil to prevent it drying.

Italian-style pork chops

2 tablespoons butter
1 tablespoon oil
450 g onions, thinly sliced
4 pork chops or steaks
a little gravy browning
½ cup Marsala (or port)
salt and pepper

Velouté sauce:
2 tablespoons flour
1 tablespoon butter
1¼ cups chicken stock
squeeze lemon juice
1 tablespoon cream

Heat the butter and oil in the frypan at 180°C (350°F) and fry the onions until soft and golden. Remove and keep warm.

Fry the chops until well-browned on both sides (about 15–20 minutes). Remove from the pan and keep warm.

While the chops are cooking, make the velouté sauce. Make a roux with the flour and butter. Cook for 3 minutes, then add the stock and bring to the boil, stirring until it is thick and smooth. Simmer gently and stir in the lemon juice and cream.

Add the velouté sauce, gravy browning and Marsala to the pan juices and boil, stirring well, until thick and smooth and reduced by one-third.

Return the onions and chops to the pan. Heat through in the sauce, season and serve with new potatoes and green vegetables.

Serves 4

Flemish pork with red cabbage

1 kg best end rib of pork, or loin
salt and pepper
good pinch mixed spice
4 tablespoons oil
1 small red cabbage, shredded
1 onion, chopped
1 clove garlic, finely chopped
½ cup vinegar
2 apples, peeled, cored and thinly sliced
1 tablespoon sugar
1 teaspoon chopped parsley
1¼ cups beef stock
1 tablespoon tomato paste
2 teaspoons cornflour, mixed with water

Preheat the oven to 190°C (375°F). Remove the rind from the pork and season with salt, pepper and mixed spice. Brush with oil and place on a rack in a roasting pan. Roast in the preheated oven for 1¼ hours, basting frequently with a cup of water.

Place the cabbage in an earthenware bowl with the onion, garlic, vinegar and 2½ cups water. Leave to stand for 15 minutes.

Add the apples to the cabbage with the sugar and seasoning. Transfer to a stainless steel pan, bring to the boil and simmer for 20 minutes.

Transfer the pork to a serving dish. Surround with the cabbage in its liquid and sprinkle with parsley.

Pour off the fat from the roasting pan, retaining the meat juices. Add the stock and tomato paste, bring to the boil and simmer for 5 minutes. Add the cornflour to the pan and simmer for 1 minute, stirring. Season and strain into a sauce boat or jug to serve.

Serves 6

Note: To save time, instead of pickling a best end or loin of pork, you can buy a gammon or back bacon joint. If you prefer, you can substitute white savoy cabbage and omit the vinegar. However, if you do use red cabbage and want to make this dish special, use red wine instead of water.

Flemish pork with red cabbage

Pork casserole

Pork casserole

This is another dish which can be stored in the freezer.

**1 kg lean leg of pork
¼ cup lard
1 onion, chopped
juice ½ lemon
1 bay leaf
2 teaspoons salt
freshly ground black pepper
1¼ cups red wine
¼ cup plain flour
1 cup chicken stock
2 tablespoons butter
100 g mushrooms, sliced
2 cloves garlic, crushed
⅝ cup white wine
300 mL sour cream**

Cut the pork into 2.5 cm cubes. Melt the lard in a large pan and gently fry the onion for 5 minutes. Add the pork, lemon juice, bay leaf, salt and pepper and half the red wine. Cover and cook gently for 15 minutes. Transfer the pork to a plate. Add the flour to the pan and stir over medium heat for 1–2 minutes. Add the remaining red wine and the stock. Stirring continuously, gradually bring the mixture to the boil.

Melt the butter in a clean pan. Add the mushrooms and crushed garlic and sauté gently for 2–3 minutes. Add the white wine, cover and simmer for 10 minutes.

Return the pork to the pan and add the mushroom mixture. Cover and simmer for 15 minutes or until the meat is tender. Check the seasoning. If you wish to serve the casserole immediately, stir in the sour cream and reheat without letting it boil.

To freeze, allow the casserole to cool before transferring it to a rigid container. Seal, label and place in the freezer. Thaw the casserole in the refrigerator before gently reheating. Stir in the sour cream and serve with creamed potatoes and braised red cabbage.

Serves 6–8

Sausage and vegetable casserole

Sausage and vegetable casserole

Most continental pork sausages are delicious simmered, baked or grilled and served hot.

They may be cut into chunks and added to soups and casseroles, chopped for sauces and stews or sliced for pizzas and quiches.

⅓ cup red kidney beans, soaked overnight
¼ small green cabbage, shredded
2 potatoes, peeled and sliced
2 carrots, peeled and chopped
1 large leek, sliced
2 onions, peeled and sliced
4 cups beef stock
salt and pepper
450g thin pork sausages

Put the kidney beans into a large saucepan with the cabbage, potatoes, carrots, leek, onion, stock and seasoning. Bring to the boil, reduce heat and simmer for 1 hour.

Twist each sausage into three to give chains of smaller sausages. Add to the casserole and simmer for a further 15 minutes, or until the sausages are cooked.

Serve with crusty bread.
Serves 4

Poultry

A good range of poultry is now readily available either fresh, frozen or smoked, whole or jointed and generally drawn, plucked and trussed ready for the oven.

As a cheap and very versatile everyday dish, chicken cannot be beaten. Chicken pieces are a convenient way to buy, particularly for soups and casseroles. But a beautifully browned and succulent whole bird is the most festive way of serving chicken for a special occasion.

Cold chicken is an easy and ever-popular picnic or buffet dish and is a great favourite with children as finger food.

The less common varieties of poultry such as duck are most impressive served at a dinner party. The rich, gamey flavour making for a memorable dish.

Remember too that the carcase of a bird need not be discarded but can be used to make an excellent stock. This can be frozen and will provide the basis for a tasty soup, sauce or casserole when needed.

Walnut chicken

This dish can be cooked ahead and frozen.

3 tablespoons oil
100 g walnut pieces
350 g chicken, cooked and cut into strips
pinch salt
1 large onion, sliced
4 celery stalks, thinly sliced
1¼ cups chicken stock
1 tablespoon cornflour
2 tablespoons dry sherry
1 teaspoon sugar
3 tablespoons soya sauce
275 g can water chestnuts, drained, and sliced
225 g can bamboo shoots, drained

Heat the oil in a pan and fry the walnuts until golden. Remove and drain. Add the chicken and fry for a few minutes. Remove and sprinkle with salt. Place the onion, celery and half the stock in the same pan and cook for 5 minutes. Mix the cornflour with the sherry, sugar, soya sauce and remaining stock. Add to the pan, stirring continuously until the sauce comes to the boil and thickens. Add the water chestnuts, bamboo shoots and walnuts with the chicken and heat through. Serve.

To freeze, allow the mixture to cool before transferring it to a rigid container. Seal, label and freeze. Thaw in the refrigerator and reheat in a pan.

Serves 4

Farmhouse potato and chicken casserole

4 chicken joints
6 tablespoons cornflour
salt and pepper
4 tablespoons butter or margarine
⅛ cup oil
900 g potatoes, peeled and quartered
4 rashers bacon, rind removed and cut into strips
½ cup mushrooms, quartered
6 spring onions
⅝ cup chicken stock
1 tablespoon chives, chopped

Preheat the oven to 190°C (375°F). Season the cornflour and use it to coat the chicken joints.

Heat the butter and oil in a pan, and fry the chicken joints until golden.

Remove the chicken from the pan and place in an ovenproof casserole with the potatoes.

Add the bacon, mushrooms and onions to the pan and fry until golden. Add to the casserole. Pour the stock into the pan and bring to the boil, stirring. Pour into the casserole. Cover the dish and bake in the preheated oven for 1 hour or until the chicken is tender.

Check the seasoning and sprinkle the finished dish with the chopped chives.

Serves 4

Poultry provides an attractive and popular meal

Provençal chicken

1 × 1.5 kg chicken
1 teaspoon salt
freshly ground black pepper
1 teaspoon butter
2 tablespoons olive oil
4 cloves garlic, peeled and cut in half
¼ teaspoon dried rosemary
½ teaspoon dried basil
¼ teaspoon dried thyme

Season the cavity of the chicken with ½ teaspoon of the salt, the pepper and butter. In a pan just large enough to hold the chicken, pour in 1 tablespoon of the oil and add the garlic. Place the chicken in the pan and sprinkle it with the remaining salt, pepper, rosemary, basil, thyme and remaining olive oil. Roast the chicken in a 220°C (425°F) oven for 1 hour, basting frequently. Remove from the pan and cut in serving pieces. Serve hot or cold.
    Serves 4

Stir-fried chicken with bamboo shoots

To conserve fuel in much Chinese cookery the ingredients are cut into small pieces and fried very quickly, stirring all the time. This is known as the stir-fry method.

1 × 1.2 kg roasting chicken, uncooked
2 small cans bamboo shoots
3 tablespoons soya or vegetable oil
4 medium onions, chopped
4 tablespoons flour
salt
½ teaspoon soya sauce
1¼ cups chicken stock
450 g mushrooms, sliced

Skin the chicken. Cut off and dice the meat.
    Drain and slice the bamboo shoots.
    Heat the oil in a large frying pan, add the onion and stir fry without browning. Add the chicken and stir fry quickly until the pieces stiffen. Sprinkle in the flour and mix well. Season with salt and soya sauce and cook for 5 minutes, stirring all the time.
    Add the stock, stir, and simmer for 15 minutes. Heat the serving dish.
    Add the mushrooms and bamboo shoots to the chicken and cook for a further 5 minutes.
    Place on the serving dish and serve at once.
    Serves 6
Note: If you can get them, use dried Chinese mushrooms in place of fresh ones. Soak 15 g dried mushrooms for 15 minutes in hot water and add them with the bamboo shoots.

Chicken with olives and mushrooms

4 chicken pieces
60 g butter
100 g bacon, cut into strips
250 g button mushrooms, washed and trimmed
1 onion, finely chopped
4 shallots, finely chopped
1 carrot, finely diced
1 tablespoon flour
1¼ cups dry white wine
3 tablespoons tomato paste
¼ teaspoon fennel seeds
salt and pepper
100 g green olives, stoned

Melt butter in large pan, add bacon and mushrooms, sauté 3 minutes. Remove from pan. Add chicken pieces to pan, cook until golden and remove.
    Fry onion, shallot and carrot until golden. Stir in flour and cook for 2 minutes, then gradually add wine, tomato paste, fennel seeds and seasoning and cook gently for 15 minutes.
    Add chicken pieces to pan, cover and simmer for 30 minutes or until tender.
    Remove cooked chicken pieces from pan and liquidise or sieve sauce. Return sauce to pan with chicken, bacon, mushrooms and olives and cook gently for 10 minutes to heat through.
    Transfer chicken and sauce to heated serving dish. Serve very hot, with creamed potatoes and a fresh green vegetable.
    Serves 4

Stir-fried chicken with bamboo shoots (and dried Chinese mushrooms

Chicken tarragon

1 × 1.5 kg chicken
1 tablespoon butter
½ teaspoon salt
freshly ground black pepper
1 teaspoon dried tarragon
2 tablespoons butter
2 carrots, diced
1 medium sized onion, finely chopped
½ cup chicken stock
½ teaspoon dried tarragon
1 tablespoon cornflour dissolved in 2 tablespoons water

Place 1 tablespoon of butter in the cavity of the chicken. Sprinkle in the salt, pepper and tarragon and truss the chicken.

Heat 2 tablespoons of butter in a heavy casserole until foaming, and brown the chicken on all sides. Remove it from the pan and set aside. If the butter is too brown, discard it and melt another 2 tablespoons of butter in the casserole.

Add the carrots and onion and cook until softened. Replace the chicken in the casserole on the bed of vegetables. Add the stock and ½ teaspoon of tarragon.

Cover with aluminium foil, then a lid and simmer slowly on top of the stove or in a 180°C (350°F) oven for 50 minutes or until chicken is tender.

Cut the chicken into serving pieces and place on a warmed platter. Thicken the pan juices with the cornflour mixture. Pour the sauce with the vegetables over the chicken and serve hot.

Serves 4

Tandoori chicken

1 × 1 kg roasting chicken
1 large onion
4 cloves garlic
½ teaspoon ground ginger
1 teaspoon coriander
1 teaspoon cumin
½ teaspoon chilli powder
2 teaspoons salt
⅔ cup plain yogurt
1 tablespoon vinegar
1 tablespoon Worcestershire sauce
2 lemons
30 g melted butter
1 teaspoon garam masala

Wash and dry the chicken, make 3 or 4 cuts on each side. Grind the onion and garlic to a paste in a blender. Add the next eight ingredients and the juice of 1 lemon, mix thoroughly. Spread mixture over chicken, marinate 5 hours.

Cook on a barbecue rotary spit or wrap in foil and barbecue over hot coals. (Chicken may also be cooked in a pre-heated oven 190°C (375°F) for 1¼–1½ hours.)

Brush with melted butter, sprinkle with garam masala and lemon juice to serve.

Serves 4

Roast duckling with stuffing

1 × 2 kg duckling
apricot stuffing or potato and onion stuffing (see following recipes)
25 mL vinegar
3 tablespoons butter
3 tablespoons clear honey
1 bunch watercress

Preheat the oven to 180°C (350°F).

Wash the duckling, dry with absorbent paper.

Spoon stuffing into the cavity of the duckling and truss securely with kitchen thread. Place on a rack in a roasting pan and prick the skin all over with a skewer, taking care not to puncture the flesh itself.

Melt the butter until just liquid but not oily.

Mix together the vinegar, butter and honey and brush all over the skin. Roast in the preheated oven for 1½ hours or until the duckling is tender. Brush the juices over the bird again 15 minutes before the end of the cooking time.

Remove the trussing thread from the duckling and leave to stand for 15–20 minutes, so the juices can settle, before carving. Place on a warmed serving platter and serve garnished with watercress.

Serves 4

Tandoori chicken

Apricot stuffing

50 g dried apricots
½ cup dry cider
1 medium onion
¼ cup margarine
1 cup breadcrumbs, fresh
1 tablespoon mint and parsley, chopped
100 g pork or beef sausage-meat or mixture of both
1 egg
salt and black pepper
pinch mace
pinch allspice

Soak the dried apricots in the cider for 2 hours, then drain, reserving the liquid. Chop the apricots and peel and chop the onion.

Heat the margarine in a pan and brown the onion slightly for 2 minutes; add the breadcrumbs and apricots, cook for 5 minutes, then remove pan from heat and cool.

Combine all the other stuffing ingredients in a bowl, together with the reserved liquid, and blend thoroughly to form a smooth but firm paste.

Use for duck, goose and guinea fowl.

Potato and onion stuffing

4 tablespoons butter or margarine
½ cup onion, chopped
175 g potatoes, cooked and diced
225 g sausage-meat
salt and pepper
1 egg
pinch sage and parsley

Heat the butter or margarine in a pan, add the onions and sauté them until tender but not brown. Add the diced cooked potato, toss together and leave to cool.

Blend the sausage-meat with salt and pepper, beaten egg and the sage and parsley. Mix in the cooled potato mixture and season to taste.

Use with all types of poultry.

Note: Always cool stuffing completely before freezing. Pack in either a polythene bag or plastic tub, seal and label. Both the apricot stuffing and potato and onion stuffing can be frozen for up to 3 months. Do not freeze stuffings which contain hard-boiled eggs or uncooked fresh fruit. Do not freeze any raw poultry which has been stuffed.

Spanish turkey casserole

6–8 turkey portions
3 cloves garlic
1 teaspoon paprika
2 teaspoons salt
black pepper, freshly ground
¾ cup vinegar
2 bay leaves
2 onions
3 tablespoons butter or margarine
4 tablespoons oil
2 cups chicken stock
2 green peppers
12 green olives
½ cup capers, drained

Skin the turkey. Peel and crush the garlic and mix together with the paprika, salt and pepper. Rub into the turkey pieces and then place in a bowl. Add vinegar and bay leaves and leave to marinate for 2 hours.

Peel and chop the onions. Heat the butter or margarine and oil in a flameproof casserole dish, add the onions and fry gently until soft. Remove from the casserole with a slotted spoon and set aside.

Drain the turkey, discard the bay leaves and add turkey to the casserole, frying gently until browned on all sides. Return the onions to the casserole, add the stock and bring to the boil.

Lower heat, cover and cook gently for about 1½ hours or until the turkey is tender when pierced with a skewer.

Fifteen minutes before the end of the cooking time, remove the cores and seeds from the peppers and slice finely. Cut the olives in half and remove the stones. Add the pepper slices and olives to the casserole with the capers and heat through. Taste, adjust the seasoning, and serve hot straight from the casserole.

Serves 6–8

Chicken liver kebabs

3 chicken breasts, boned
6 rashers streaky bacon
½ green pepper
½ red pepper
12 small onions
6 button mushrooms
1 small firm tomato
12 chicken livers
6 fresh bay leaves
juice 1 lemon
2 tablespoons oil

Stretch the bacon rashers with the back of a knife and cut each one in half. Cut the chicken meat into 2.5 cm cubes. Cut the green and red pepper into 2.5 cm squares. Peel the onions and halve the mushrooms. Cut the tomato into 6 wedges. Clean the chicken livers and wrap each one in a piece of bacon.

Thread the prepared ingredients and the bay leaves alternately on to 6 long skewers. Season the kebabs and brush with lemon juice and oil. Grill for 15 minutes, turning frequently and brushing with lemon juice and oil.

Arrange the kebabs on a bed of boiled rice and serve hot, with salad.

Serves 6

Chicken liver kebabs

Vegetable dishes and salads

Too many animal fats in the diet are now thought to contribute to the high incidence of heart disease in the western world; as a consequence there is a growing awareness of the important role of vegetables in a healthy, balanced diet.

In Australia we are fortunate in having access to a wide range of fresh vegetables all year round; there are many high quality canned and frozen brands available as well. Apart from their nutritive value vegetables are colourful and interesting in texture and can make a meal look as good as it tastes. So for delicious, healthy and attractive meals try some of these quick and easy recipes.

Celery mornay

This is a good cook-ahead recipe for the freezer.

2 heads celery
salt
2 tablespoons butter
¼ cup flour
2½ cups milk
pepper
1 teaspoon made mustard
1½ cups cheese, grated
100g lean bacon, chopped (optional)

Prepare the celery: remove the leaves and outer sticks and cut the heads in half lengthways. Place in salted water and bring to the boil. Simmer for 10 minutes until tender but not soft.

Meanwhile, melt the butter in a pan. Stir in the flour and cook for 1 minute. Remove the pan from the heat and stir in the milk little by little, beating to make a smooth sauce. Add the pepper and mustard. Return to the heat and bring to the boil. Stir in the cheese until it is completely blended and the sauce is thick but not stiff.

Drain the celery and place it in a serving dish. Pour the sauce over the top. If wished, grill or fry the bacon until crisp, and scatter over the dish.

If the dish is to be served at once, place it under the grill for 5–10 minutes until the top is golden brown.

To freeze: cover the dish with foil, seal, label, and freeze. When required, thaw for 12 hours in a refrigerator. Preheat the oven to 180°C (350°F), and bake the dish, uncovered, for 20–30 minutes until heated through. Finish off under the grill to brown the top.

Serves 4

Celery mornay

ringtime salad (See page 71)

Broccoli in caper sauce

1 bunch broccoli
1 cup buttermilk
2 tablespoons cornflour
1 cup yogurt
salt and pepper
2 teaspoons capers, chopped
½ teaspoon turmeric
4 tablespoons sour cream

Trim broccoli stalks and slit from base to flower. Stand broccoli in boiling salted water and cook until stalks are just tender, about 8 minutes. Drain and cover to keep warm while preparing sauce.

Blend buttermilk with cornflour and heat in saucepan, stirring occasionally. Add yoghurt, salt, pepper, capers and turmeric. Stir until mixture thickens. Add sour cream to thin down sauce. Place broccoli on serving plate, spoon some sauce over for garnish and serve remainder separately.

Serves 4

Asparagus au gratin

1 kg thick asparagus spears
4 tomatoes
½ cup cheese, grated
1 tablespoon parsley, chopped
salt and pepper
4 tablespoons butter

Wash the asparagus. Trim any tough parts from the thick end of the stalks, and scrape the stems lightly with a potato peeler. Tie in bundles of about 8 stalks and boil for 15 minutes in salted water.

Preheat the oven to 200°C (400°F).

Drain the asparagus and arrange the spears in rows in a lightly greased, ovenproof dish.

Slice the tomatoes, and lay the slices in overlapping rows between the asparagus heads. Sprinkle with the cheese and parsley. Season with salt and pepper and bake in the oven for 10 minutes. Melt the butter and pour over the dish before serving.

Note: The inedible, tough ends of asparagus stalks, together with the cooking water, can be used to make a delicious soup. Just blend with an equal quantity of white sauce and a little chopped ham. Pureé the mixture and season to taste.

Serves 8

Asparagus au gratin

Tomato pie

1 packet frozen shortcrust pastry
6–8 medium-sized tomatoes
2 tablespoons chives, chopped
2 tablespoons cornflour
1½ tablespoons sugar
salt and pepper
beaten egg

Set the oven at 200°C (400°F). Roll out two-thirds of the pastry and use to line a 20 cm flan dish.

Slice the tomatoes. Mix the chives, cornflour and sugar with seasoning to taste. Put a layer of sliced tomatoes in the pastry case and sprinkle with the chive mixture. Continue to layer the tomatoes, sprinkling the chive mixture between the layers.

Roll out the remaining pastry and use to cover the pie, sealing the edges with a little water. Trim the pastry edge and flute. Decorate with 'leaves' made from pastry trimmings.

Brush the pie with a little beaten egg and bake for 40–45 minutes, until golden-brown. Serve hot or cold, with cold meat or salad.

Serves 6–8

Stuffed vine leaves

16 vine leaves, canned or fresh
1.2 L chicken stock
juice of 1 lemon and rind, grated
salt

Stuffing:
2 cups long-grain rice, cooked
⅓ cup sultanas
1 tablespoon grated onion
½ cup walnuts, chopped
50 g mushrooms, chopped
salt and pepper
1 teaspoon dill, chopped
1 tablespoon allspice

Preheat the oven to 190°C (275°F).

If using fresh vine leaves, boil in salted water for 4 minutes.

Mix together all the stuffing ingredients in a bowl.

Place a spoonful of the stuffing on each vine leaf, roll up each into a small parcel and arrange in an ovenproof dish.

Bring stock to the boil and add the lemon juice, grated rind and salt. Cover the vine leaves with the stock and bake in the oven (with the lid on) for 35 minutes. Garnish with lemon slices and serve.

Serves 4

Stuffed vine leaves

Tomato pie

Onions in cream sauce

sea salt
18 medium onions
6 tablespoons butter
1 tablespoon sugar
½ cup dry white wine
1 cup thick cream
salt and pepper
pinch ginger
few sprigs chervil, chopped

Bring a large pan of water to the boil. Add a handful of sea salt.
　Peel the onions, without cutting off the root end. Drop them into the boiling water and simmer 5–10 minutes or until they begin to soften. Drain.
　Melt the butter in a heavy-based saucepan. Add the onions. Sprinkle them with the sugar and let them caramelise, turning gently with a wooden spoon without breaking them.
　When the onions are evenly and well browned put them in a heated serving dish and keep hot. Pour the wine into the saucepan. Stir quickly to mix with the caramelised juices. Stir in the cream and let the sauce thicken over a low heat, stirring constantly.
　Season to taste with salt, pepper and ginger. Pour this sauce over the onions.
　Sprinkle the onions with the chervil and serve very hot.
　Serves 6

Mushroom flan

225 g shortcrust pastry
2 tablespoons butter
1 small onion, finely chopped
225 g mushrooms, finely chopped
salt
black pepper, freshly ground
1 tablespoon chopped parsley
1 tablespoon flour
2 eggs, beaten
1¼ cups milk

Preheat the oven to 200°C (400°F).
　Roll out the pastry to a thickness of 5 mm. Line a 20 cm flan tin with it. Prick evenly with a fork and leave to rest in a cool place.
　Heat the butter in a frying pan. Gently fry the onion for 5 minutes until it is soft but not brown, then add the mushrooms and cook for 1 minute. Season with salt, pepper and parsley. Leave the mixture to cool.
　In a mixing bowl, beat the flour, eggs and milk. Stir in the onion and mushroom mixture.
　Pour the filling into the flan tin. Bake for 30 minutes in the oven. Serve hot or cold.
　Serves 6
Note: Flans should look as attractive as possible; their presentation is as important as their flavour. Arrange button mushrooms around the edge to make a decorative border.
　Herbs and spices can complement the mushroom flavour beautifully. Use tarragon or chervil, or add some crushed garlic or powdered cloves.

Mushroom flan

Spinach turnovers

450 g puff pastry
675 g spinach, frozen and thawed
¾ cup grated Cheddar cheese
pinch nutmeg
salt and pepper
2 egg yolks beaten
juice 1 lemon
1 egg, beaten
1 tablespoon sesame seeds

Preheat the oven to 200°C (400°F).

Roll out the pastry 3 mm thick. Using a round pastry cutter, cut out circles of 10 cm diameter.

Drain the spinach and squeeze to extract as much water as possible, then chop finely. Place in a bowl and add the cheese and nutmeg and season with salt and pepper. Add the egg yolks and lemon juice and mix well.

Divide the spinach mixture between the pastry circles. Brush the edges of the pastry with a little water. Fold the pastry over the spinach and press the edges together firmly.

Brush the pastry circles with the beaten egg and sprinkle with sesame seeds.

Place the turnovers on a greased baking tray and bake for 20 minutes.

Serves 6–8

Tomatoes Roquefort

4 tomatoes
1 onion
1 tablespoon parsley, chopped
½ cup Roquefort cheese
2 tablespoons olive oil
2 tablespoons lemon juice
1 teaspoon sugar
salt
pepper
paprika

Wash tomatoes, slice thinly and place on serving platter. Peel onion, slice very thinly and place rings of onion over tomatoes.

Blend all remaining ingredients until creamy and pour over vegetables. Chill before serving.

Serves 4

Crab and raisin salad

100 g long grain rice
500 g crabmeat
1 green pepper, shredded
50 g raisins
25 g walnuts, chopped
2 teaspoons chopped celery leaves
1 teaspoon chopped chives
good pinch paprika
salt and pepper

Dressing:
3 tablespoons oil
1½ tablespoons lemon juice
pinch dry mustard
pinch sugar

Cook the rice in boiling salted water for about 15 minutes. Drain, rinse in cold water and drain again. Leave to cool.

Mix the rice with the remaining salad ingredients and season to taste.

Beat together the dressing ingredients, pour over the salad and toss lightly. Serve on a bed of lettuce.

Serves 4–6

Springtime salad

3 cups cauliflorets
1 avocado
lemon juice
1 cup asparagus pieces
1 lettuce
salt
¼ cup chopped shallots
2 tablespoons olive oil
4 tablespoons tarragon vinegar
1 teaspoon chopped parsley
salt and pepper
¼ teaspoon mustard
sesame seeds

Steam cauliflorets until tender but still crisp. Refresh under cold water, pat dry.
Halve avocado, remove seed and peel. Cube, sprinkle with lemon juice to prevent browning.
Cover asparagus with boiling salted water, cook 5 minutes, refresh under cold water, and pat dry.
Wash lettuce. Combine florets, avocado, asparagus and shallots. Chill.
Combine oil, vinegar, parsley, salt, pepper and mustard; pour over salad, toss and serve garnished with toasted sesame seeds in a glass bowl lined with lettuce leaves. Try using cos lettuce for a change.
Serves 6

Macaroni and zucchini salad

250 g zucchini
salt
1 cup sliced mushrooms
1 cup cooked wholemeal macaroni
¾ cup cream
¼ cup crunchy peanut butter
½ cup mayonnaise
1 tablespoon honey
1 tablespoon white vinegar
2 tablespoons lemon juice
½ cup roasted peanuts

Wash and slice zucchini. Place on kitchen paper, sprinkle with salt and allow to stand 30 minutes. Rinse under cold water and pat dry. Combine zucchini, mushrooms and macaroni in salad bowl. Chill while preparing dressing.
Place all remaining ingredients except peanuts in blender and whip until smooth but not too thick. Coat salad lightly with dressing. Chill well and serve garnished with roasted peanuts. The extra dressing will keep well in refrigerator.
Serves 6

Potato and celery salad

1 small onion
6 large lettuce leaves
450 g boiled new potatoes, cold and sliced
1¼ cups sliced celery
1¼ cups green peas, cooked
150 mL yogurt
1 tablespoon horseradish cream
juice 1 lemon
salt and pepper
12 capers

Peel the onion and cut it into thin rings.
Wash and drain the lettuce leaves.
Mix together the potatoes, celery and peas in a bowl.
Blend together the yogurt, horseradish cream, lemon juice, and seasoning and mix with the vegetables.
Arrange in a shallow dish, dot with capers and decorate with lettuce leaves.
Serves 6

Macaroni and zucchini salad

Pasta and rice

RICE has been a staple food in Asia for centuries but has only become widely popular in the west in comparatively recent times. There are many different varieties of rice which may be bought husked and polished (white rice) or unpolished with only the outer husk removed (brown rice). Brown rice requires a longer cooking time and has a chewy texture and slightly nutty flavour. Bearing these facts in mind brown rice may be substituted for white in any of the given recipes.

Pasta is also a very ancient dish. The Chinese were making it 6000 years ago and European explorers introduced it to the west. The Italians have now made pasta their national dish.

Both rice and pasta provide a substantial element of starch in a meal. As well as being tasty in themselves they serve as excellent 'padding' if other ingredients are in short supply. Rice and pasta provide essential carbohydrates and make a healthy and welcome change to predominantly meat meals.

Bolognese sauce and spaghetti

¼ cup oil
1 onion, chopped
1 stick celery, chopped
1 clove garlic, chopped
225 g minced beef
¼ cup minced chicken or calves' liver
4 tablespoons flour
2 tablespoons tomato paste
1¼ cups beef stock
¼ cup dark sherry or Marsala
pinch each oregano, paprika and mace
salt and pepper

Heat the oil in a pan and sauté the onion, celery and garlic for 5 minutes until lightly browned.

Add the minced beef and liver and cook for a further 5 minutes.

Sprinkle in the flour and cook for 1 minute. Stir in the tomato paste and cook for 1 minute more. Add beef stock with the sherry or Marsala. Add the oregano, paprika, mace and seasoning and simmer for a further 15 minutes. Can be served with a garnish of black olives.

Makes ½ litre of sauce.

Tips for cooking spaghetti
As with all pasta, the length of cooking time depends upon the texture you prefer. Add the spaghetti to plenty of boiling salted water. Ten minutes produces spaghetti which is just cooked but still firm (*al dente*), while cooking for 15 minutes will make the pasta quite soft. Drain well.

To serve, sprinkle the pasta with grated cheese. Parmesan is the usual choice because it is so dry, but other hard cheeses such as Cheddar and Gruyère can also be used. For the best results, grate cheese which has been left unwrapped in the refrigerator for a few days and is very dry.

Bolognese sauce and spaghetti

Spaghetti Amalfi

3 eggplants, diced
salt
¼ cup oil
1 onion, chopped
1 clove garlic, peeled and chopped
1 green pepper, seeded and diced
2 mushrooms, sliced
4 tablespoons flour
2 tablespoons tomato paste
⅝ cup chicken stock
pinch each basil, paprika, curry powder
pepper
225 g spaghetti
2 tablespoons butter
½ cup cheese, grated

Sprinkle the diced eggplants with salt and leave to stand for 30 minutes. Rinse and dry.

Heat the oil in a pan and fry the onion and garlic for 5 minutes without browning. Add the pepper, eggplant and mushrooms and simmer for 3 minutes more. Sprinkle in the flour and add the tomato paste and stock. Add the basil, paprika, curry powder, salt and pepper. Simmer for 12 minutes.

Meanwhile, cook the spaghetti in salted water, drain and add the butter and grated cheese. Mix well.

Place the spaghetti on a serving dish, cover with the eggplant sauce and serve.

Serves 4

Lasagne al Forno

Lasagne is the name given to flat sheets (about 13 cm square) or very wide strips of pasta. It may be white, brown (wholemeal) or green (spinach-flavoured) and is usually cooked in layers with meat sauce and topped with grated cheese.

3 tablespoons oil
1 onion, chopped
2 cloves garlic, crushed
700 g tomatoes, peeled and finely chopped
½ green pepper, finely chopped
1 bay leaf
sprig parsley
pinch each oregano and basil
salt and pepper
350 g spinach
350 g Ricotta or curd cheese
25 g Parmesan cheese, grated
2 eggs, beaten
1 tablespoon chopped parsley
250 g white or green lasagne
100 g Mozzarella or Gruyère cheese,
 coarsely grated

Heat the oil and fry the onion and garlic until soft. Add the tomatoes, pepper, herbs and seasoning and simmer for 30 minutes, adding a little water if necessary.

Set the oven at 180°C (350°F). Wash and chop the spinach and mix with the Ricotta, Parmesan, beaten eggs, parsley and seasoning. Cook the lasagne in boiling salted water for 10–15 minutes, and drain well.

Butter a square baking dish. Arrange a layer of lasagne in the base of the dish, spread with some of the spinach mixture, sprinkle with Mozzarella or Gruyère and cover with the tomato sauce. Repeat the layers once or twice. Cover securely with aluminium foil and bake for 40 minutes. Remove the foil and bake for a further 10–15 minutes.

Serve hot with herb bread and a crisp green salad.

Serves 4–6

Cannelloni with olives

Cannelloni with olives

Cannelloni are hollow pasta tubes, usually about 10 cm long and 5 cm in diameter. They can be stuffed with a variety of meat, cheese or vegetable mixtures.

Cannelloni can be served either as an appetiser or as a main course with a green salad.

6 tubes cannelloni
1 tablespoon oil
1 onion, chopped
225 g minced beef
1 tablespoon tomato paste
1 teaspoon basil
1 teaspoon sugar
8 stuffed olives
salt and pepper
1 tomato, thinly sliced

Sauce:
1¼ cups white sauce
½ teaspoon made mustard
salt and pepper
1 cup grated cheese

Blanch the cannelloni in a pan of salted boiling water for 5 minutes. Drain and place under running cold water until cool.

Heat the oven to 190°C (375°F).

Heat the oil in a frying pan and fry the onion until soft. Add the minced beef and cook until brown. Stir in the tomato paste, basil and sugar.

Chop 6 olives, add them to the mixture and season with salt and pepper.

Using a piping bag or spoon, fill the cannelloni tubes with the mixture. Place in a shallow ovenproof dish.

Heat the white sauce and flavour with mustard, salt and pepper. Stir in most of the cheese, reserving a little for the top.

Pour the sauce over the cannelloni and sprinkle with the remaining cheese. Bake in the oven for 20 minutes.

Decorate the top with the remaining sliced olives and tomato and serve hot.

Serves 3–6

Note: This dish can be served as an appetiser, in which case allow one cannelloni tube per person. If serving as a main course, allow two per person.

Cauliflower and macaroni soufflé

Macaroni is another popular, pipe-shaped pasta.

1 medium cauliflower
2 teaspoons made mustard
3 eggs, separated
salt and pepper
1¼ cups white sauce
1 cup grated cheese
100 g short macaroni, cooked

Break up the washed, trimmed cauliflower into florets and cut the stalks into small pieces. Boil until tender in salted water. Drain and mash to a purée. Add the mustard and egg yolks, and seasoning.

Preheat the oven to 190°C (375°F).

To give the soufflé a good start and help it rise rapidly while cooking, lay a baking sheet on the middle shelf when you preheat the oven. Put your soufflé dish on this baking sheet.

Add half of the grated cheese to the white sauce, away from the heat. When cold add to the purée.

Mix in the cooked macaroni.

Beat the egg whites until stiff and fold in gently. Spoon into a greased ovenproof dish or soufflé dish and bake for 35–40 minutes until well-risen and golden. Serve immediately. Can be garnished with watercress.

Serves 4

Note: Another way used by chefs to give the soufflé a good start is to place it in a roasting pan of hot water on top of the stove for 5 minutes, and then carefully to put it into the oven to continue baking.

Frankfurts and noodles

There is a great variety of noodles, especially in Italian cooking, ranging from tagliatelle, about 2 cm wide to fettuccine around 5 mm wide.

Most need to be cooked for about 8 minutes and it is a good idea to add a few drops of oil to the cooking water to stop them from sticking.

225 g noodles
2½ cups fresh or thawed frozen peas
4 tablespoons butter
275 g frozen or fresh spinach, cooked and drained
450 g frankfurt sausages, sliced
300 mL cream of mushroom soup
½ cup sour cream
½ cup milk
4 rashers bacon, cooked and crumbled

Preheat the oven to 200°C (400°F).

Boil the noodles in salted water for 8 minutes. Drain and mix with half the peas and the butter.

Grease the inside of a casserole. Place the cooked spinach in a layer on the bottom. Spoon the noodle mixture over the spinach. Mix the frankfurts with the soup, sour cream and milk. Pour over the noodles. Bake for 20 minutes then sprinkle the rest of the peas and the bacon over the surface and cook for another 5 minutes.

Serves 4

Frankfurts and noodles

Cauliflower and macaroni soufflé

Dolmades

8 cabbage leaves
450 g minced beef
1 medium onion, chopped
¼ cup oil
50 g rice, cooked
1 teaspoon mixed herbs
salt and pepper
1¼ cups fresh tomato sauce (see recipe in 'Soups, sauces and garnishes' chapter)

Preheat the oven to 180°C (350°F).

Boil the cabbage leaves in salted water for 5 minutes. Drain and dry on absorbent paper.

Gently fry the mince and chopped onion in the oil until the meat is brown (about 10 minutes).

Add the cooked rice, herbs and seasoning.

Divide the filling between the cabbage leaves, roll up and arrange close together in a baking dish just big enough to hold them. Pour the tomato sauce over, cover with a lid, and bake for 40 minutes. Serve hot as an appetiser or as a main dish with plain, boiled rice.

Serves 4

Note: Traditional Greek dolmades consist of lamb wrapped in vine leaves, blanched for 5 minutes and flavoured with mint. You can buy vine leaves in cans in delicatessens or fresh ones may be used.

Rice pilaff

4 tablespoons butter
3 tablespoons oil
1 small onion, chopped
175 g patna rice
salt and freshly ground black pepper
1⅞ cups chicken stock

Heat the butter and oil in a saucepan and fry the onion gently for 2 minutes.

Add the rice and stir for 1 minute until it is translucent. Season.

Add the stock. Bring to the boil and transfer to an ovenproof dish covered with a lid.

Bake for 15–18 minutes until the rice is cooked and fluffy.

Serves 4–6

Country chicken risotto

2 tablespoons oil
4 tablespoons butter
1 onion, chopped
¾ cup long grain rice
1 cup cooked chicken, diced
1 clove garlic, chopped
1⅞ cups chicken stock
salt and pepper
pinch dried basil
2 tomatoes, skinned, seeded and chopped
½ cup cooked green peas
½ cup cheese, grated

Heat the oil and half the butter together in a frying pan and fry the onion gently, without browning, for 4 minutes. Stir in the rice and cook for 4 minutes or until the rice become opaque.

Add the cooked chicken, garlic and chicken stock and season with salt and pepper and basil. Bring to the boil, cover with a lid and cook gently for 20 minutes or until the rice is tender. Check from time to time to make sure the rice is not sticking to the pan, adding a little water if necessary.

Remove from heat and stir in the chopped tomato and cooked peas. Turn the rice mixture into a heated serving dish and sprinkle cheese over the top. Put the dish under the grill for a minute to melt the cheese. Serve immediately.

Serves 4

Note: This dish may be varied by adding ½ cup diced cooked ham, corn kernels or chopped mushrooms. Garnish with 1 tablespoon chopped fresh parsley.

A more meaty-tasting risotto can be made using the same recipe, but substituting for the chicken ½ cup chopped chicken liver and the same amount of diced bacon, and frying 2 minutes before adding the other ingredients.

Tomatoes stuffed with rice

Using rice in stuffings is a good way to add carbohydrate and nutrients. The rice used must always be at least half cooked and some fat should be included in the stuffing ingredients so that the rice grains remain separate and do not become sticky.

12 large, firm tomatoes
2 teaspoons sugar
salt and pepper
½ cup oil
2 onions, chopped
1 bunch parsley, chopped
1⅜ cups long grain rice
2 tablespoons currants
2 tablespoons pine nuts
2 tablespoons dried breadcrumbs

Preheat the oven to 200°C (400°F). Cut a lid from the stalk end of each tomato and scoop out their centres. Discard the seeds and dice the pulp. Sprinkle the insides of the tomatoes with sugar, salt and pepper.

Heat 4 tablespoons of the oil in a pan and cook the onion until softened. Add the parsley and tomato pulp and cook over a low heat until most of the moisture has evaporated.

Meanwhile, cook the rice in boiling salted water.

Add the currants and pine nuts to the rice. Add the onion and tomato mixture.

Fill the tomatoes with the rice mixture. Place them in an ovenproof dish and sprinkle with the breadcrumbs and the rest of the oil. Bake in the oven for 15 minutes and serve hot.

Serves 6

Spanish seafood paella

This may be coooked in an electric frypan.

1.5 kg boiling chicken, cooked
¼ cup olive oil
1 onion, chopped
2 cloves garlic, crushed
1 red pepper, seeded and sliced
1½ cups long-grain rice
225 g peas, shelled
550 mL mussels
1 cup peeled, cooked prawns
chicken stock
juice ½ lemon
1 bay leaf
salt and pepper
pinch saffron
6 king prawns, uncooked
1 tablespoon butter, melted
1 tablespoon lemon juice
8 stuffed olives, sliced

Remove the chicken flesh and cut into chunks or strips. Heat the oil in a frypan or an electric frypan set at 170°C (325°F), and fry the onion and garlic until transparent. Add the red pepper and sauté until soft.

Stir in the rice and fry until it is a pale golden colour. Add the shelled peas, mussels, prawns and chicken. Pour in enough chicken stock to completely cover the ingredients in the pan. Add the lemon juice and bay leaf, cover with the lid and lower the heat or reduce the temperature on the electric frypan to 110°C (225°F). Cook until the rice is tender and all of the liquid has been absorbed. Season to taste and stir in the saffron, mixing it well so that the rice is evenly coloured.

While the rice is cooking grill the king prawns, brushing them occasionally with melted butter and lemon juice.

Transfer the paella to a serving dish and garnish with the grilled prawns and sliced stuffed olives.

Serves 6–8

Curried brown rice salad

3 cups cooked brown rice
½ cup diced red pepper
½ cup tinned corn kernels
½ cup chopped spring onions
salt and pepper
¼ cup chopped celery
1 tablespoon salad oil
2 tablespoons tarragon vinegar
1 teaspoon parsley, chopped
2 teaspoons curry powder

Combine rice, capsicum, corn, spring onions, salt, pepper and celery in a salad bowl. Mix oil, vinegar, parsley and curry powder, pour over salad and toss.

For a party increase quantities and place in separate bowls. Prepare dressing, coat rice, capsicum, corn and spring onions lightly with dressing and toss. Layer in large glass salad bowl and chill before serving. Served in this way it makes a spectacular party dish.

Serves 6

Baked fish with parsley rice

1 cup long-grain rice
2½ cups water
1 teaspoon salt
2 tablespoons chopped parsley
6 tablespoons butter or margarine
675 g tomatoes, peeled and chopped
salt and pepper
pinch nutmeg
450 g white fish
pinch garlic salt
pinch basil
1 cup fresh breadcrumbs

Preheat the oven to 200°C (400°F).

Put the rice, water and salt in a pan, bring to the boil and stir once. Lower the heat to a simmer, cover and cook for 15 minutes or until the rice is tender and all the liquid has been absorbed.

Add the chopped parsley and 2 tablespoons of the butter or margarine to the rice and mix well.

Grease an ovenproof dish with 2 tablespoons of the butter or margarine and place half the rice in the bottom. Cover with half the tomatoes and season with salt, pepper and nutmeg.

Cut the fish into small thin slices and place on top of the tomatoes. Season with salt, pepper, garlic salt and basil, cover with the remaining tomatoes and rice.

Season the breadcrumbs and sprinkle them over the top. Dot with the rest of the butter or margarine and cover with foil. Bake in preheated oven for 20 minutes.

Remove the foil and place under a hot grill for 2–3 minutes until browned on top.

Serves 6

Note: Fish and rice make a delicious combination and to obtain maximum flavour, cook the rice in fish stock.

The fish can also be cooked in the stock or together in the same pan with the rice. If the fish is in large pieces place it on a bed of rice and cook the two for the same length of time. If the fish is in small pieces however, add them to the pan about ten minutes before the rice has finished cooking.

Curried brown rice salad

Desserts

ALTHOUGH not a daily occurrence in most busy families desserts make a delightful dénouement to a well-balanced meal. Among the easiest, healthiest and most decorative desserts is fresh fruit. A bowl of fruit served unaccompanied at the end of a rich meal looks spectacular and tastes delicious and refreshing. To add a sophisticated touch practically any fruit can be macerated in brandy, rum or liqueur and topped with a swirl of whipped cream.

Jellies, bavaroises, soufflés and cream desserts make a richer but light end to a meal. They are cool and refreshing which makes them most welcome in summer.

French flans — crème pâtissière and fruit in shortcrust pastry case — are quite easy to make but taste and look special.

To balance a light main course a sweet pie or a rich cake may be served or one of the classic creamy French custards such as Crème Caramel.

Crème caramel

2 tablespoons water
100 g sugar cubes
4 eggs
¼ cup sugar
4 drops vanilla essence
2½ cups milk

Make the caramel by bringing half of the water and the sugar cubes to the boil in a heavy-based saucepan. When they begin to caramelise, add the remaining water and reboil until the water and caramel mix.

Line the mould as shown in the illustration.

Preheat the oven to 180°C (350°F). Cream together the eggs, sugar and vanilla essence. Heat the milk, without letting it boil, and gradually whisk it into the egg mixture. Strain and pour into the mould. Place the mould in a roasting pan, half-filled with water and bake for 1 hour, or until set.

Chill thoroughly before turning out on to a serving dish. Pour any caramel remaining in the mould around the dish and serve.

Serves 6

Banana rum bavarois

1¼ cups milk
¼ cup sugar
4 egg yolks, beaten
¼ cup powdered gelatine
3 bananas, sieved
1¼ cups cream, whipped
1 teaspoon rum

Heat the milk and sugar in a pan and pour it gradually on to the egg yolks. Return to the pan and heat, stirring constantly, until the mixture is thick and creamy, taking care not to boil. Pour into a basin and leave to cool.

Melt the gelatine in a little warm water and add to the custard along with the banana purée.

Beat the cream until stiff and mix in the rum. Add this to the custard and mix well. Pour into a moistened mould and leave to set. Turn on to a dish and serve.

Serves 4–6

Banana mousse

450 g bananas
1 tablespoon lemon juice
2 tablespoons soft brown sugar
⅝ cup yogurt
4 tablespoons thick cream
2 egg whites
1 tablespoon flaked almonds
demerara sugar for serving
shortbread biscuits for serving

Skin the bananas and chop roughly. Put them in a blender with all the remaining ingredients except the egg whites, almonds and demerara sugar and blend until smooth. Turn the mixture into a bowl.

Whisk the egg whites until stiff and fold them with the almonds into the mixture. Turn into a serving dish. Cover and chill until the mousse thickens and darkens slightly. Sprinkle with demerara sugar and serve with shortbread biscuits.

Serves 4

trus sherbet cups (See page 87)

Rum and chocolate mousse

A cold sweet mousse is similar to a cold soufflé but has a creamier, less fluffy texture.

You can make this mousse ahead and store it in the freezer.

175 g plain chocolate
3 tablespoons rum
2 tablespoons water
2 eggs, separated
few drops vanilla essence
³⁄₈ cup caster sugar
2½ cups cream, whipped

Line a 20 cm soufflé dish with greaseproof paper. Melt the chocolate with the rum and water in a bowl over a pan of hot water.

Remove the bowl from the heat and mix in the egg yolks and vanilla essence. Cool.

Whisk the egg whites until they form soft peaks, then fold in the sugar, a spoonful at a time. Stir the meringue into the chocolate mixture.

Place the cream in a bowl and whip until it forms peaks. Fold into the chocolate meringue mixture. Pour the mousse into the prepared soufflé dish and place in the freezer until firm. Put it in a polythene bag, seal and label before returning to the freezer.

To serve, thaw the mousse at room temperature for 30 minutes and decorate with chocolate curls and piped cream.

Serves 4

Apricot whip

This recipe and the following one for 'Banana and chocolate egg nog' can be easily made in a blender.

225 g canned apricots
1 teaspoon powdered gelatine
¼ cup syrup from the apricots, warmed
juice ½ lemon
2 tablespoons gin
1¼ cups thick cream
1 tablespoon grated chocolate

Place the apricots in a blender and purée.

Dissolve the gelatine in the warmed apricot syrup and mix with the purée. Add the lemon juice, gin and half the cream. Blend again lightly.

Whip the remaining cream and fold it into the apricot mixture. Pour the mixture into 4 serving glasses and refrigerate for 2 hours or until set. Sprinkle with grated chocolate and serve.

Serves 6

Strawberry de luxe

Bavarois, or Bavarian cream, is based on an egg and milk custard to which gelatine and cream are added to set it and make it creamy. It was invented by a French chef who lived in Bavaria.

6 small sponge fingers
¼ cup kirsch
175 g strawberries, washed and hulled
⅝ cup water
½ cup caster sugar
1 tablespoon powdered gelatine
juice ½ lemon
⅝ cup cream, lightly whipped

Cut the sponge fingers into pieces 2.5 cm long and place them in a bowl. Pour over the kirsch and let them soak for 1 hour.

Put aside 6 strawberries for garnishing. Purée the rest either in a blender or by forcing them through a sieve.

In a saucepan heat the water and stir in the sugar until it dissolves. Allow this syrup to cool.

Dissolve the gelatine in 2 tablespoons of warm water. In a bowl combine the strawberry purée, syrup and lemon juice and stir in the gelatine. Lastly fold in the whipped cream.

Wet a 900 mL fluted mould with a little water and pour in the bavarois mixture. Arrange the sponge pieces over the top so that the surface is compactly covered. Chill in the refrigerator until set solid.

Dip the mould in hot water and turn the bavarois out on a serving dish. Garnish with the reserved strawberries and serve.

Serves 6–8

Raspberry soufflé

This soufflé can be prepared ahead and put in the freezer.

oil for greasing
450 g raspberries, fresh or frozen and thawed
4 eggs separated
½ cup caster sugar
⅝ cup cream, whipped
2 teaspoons powdered gelatine
5 tablespoons water

To serve:
3 tablespoons chopped nuts
⅝ cup cream, whipped
5 walnut halves
4 raspberries

Tie a double band of greaseproof paper around a 15 cm soufflé dish. Lightly oil the inside of the paper.

Purée the raspberries. Add the egg yolks and sugar to the purée and whisk until thick and mousse-like. Fold in the cream.

Place the gelatine and water in a bowl and leave to soften for 5 minutes. Stand the bowl in a pan of hot water and stir until the gelatine has dissolved. Stir into the raspberry mixture.

When the mixture begins to set, stiffly whisk the egg whites and fold in carefully with a large metal spoon. Turn the mixture into the prepared soufflé dish and leave in a cool place to set.

If you wish to freeze the soufflé, place it, uncovered, in the freezer until firm. Wrap it with aluminium foil, place in a thick polythene bag, seal, label and freeze.

Thaw the frozen soufflé in the refrigerator for 8–10 hours.

To serve, remove the paper collar and press the chopped nuts on to the sides. Pipe a border of whipped cream around the top and decorate with the walnut halves and raspberries.

Serves 6

Citrus sherbet cups

2 bananas, peeled
2 eggs, separated
2 cups caster sugar
¾ cup orange juice
¼ cup lemon juice
2 cups grapefruit and pineapple juice, mixed
450 g green grapes, peeled

Mash the bananas and mix in the egg yolks and sugar.

Stiffly whisk the egg whites and fold into the banana mixture.

Stir in the fruit juices and pour the mixture into a freezer tray. Freeze until firm, whisking the mixture from time to time.

Spoon the mixture into glasses and top with grapes.

Serves 4

Raspberry soufflé

Pineapple flambé

Pineapple flambé

This dish is spectacular if cooked at the table, in front of your guests, over a spirit burner.

You can substitute other spirits or liqueurs for brandy, such as rum, kirsch, Cointreau or crème de framboises.

1 fresh pineapple
4 tablespoons butter
2 tablespoons clear honey
¼ cup brown sugar
6–8 glacé cherries
½ cup brandy

Cut the pineapple into 6–8 slices and remove the outer skin.

Melt the butter, honey and brown sugar in a large frying pan and sauté the pineapple until it softens and the liquid becomes syrupy. Place a glacé cherry in the centre of each pineapple slice.

Add the brandy and set it alight. Serve the pineapple flambé flaming, if possible. You can extinguish the flames by covering the pan with a lid. Serve with whipped cream.

Serves 4–8

Lime trifle

4 trifle sponges
2 tablespoons jam
100g canned mandarin segments in juice
100g canned pineapple chunks in juice
1½ packets lime jelly
½ cup cream, whipped

Split the trifle sponges and sandwich together again with the jam. Quarter the sandwiches and place in a serving dish.

Drain the canned fruit, reserving the juice. Make the juice up to 2¾ cups with water, and use to make the lime jelly.

Pour a little of the jelly over the sponges and refrigerate until completely set.

Mix the fruit with the remaining jelly and pour over the set jelly and sponge. Return to the refrigerator to set.

Whip the cream until just thick and pipe on to the jelly.

Serves 8

Fresh fruit ice-cream

This recipe is suitable for any type of fresh fruit. Soft fruit should be freshly sieved and hard fruit cooked, cooled and sieved. For 2½ cups of fruit pulp you will need about 1 kg stoneless fruits (strawberries, raspberries, cranberries, gooseberries, etc.), and a little more for fruits with stones.

2½ cups fresh fruit pulp
juice ½ lemon
juice ½ orange
1 cup sugar
⅝ cup water
⅝ cup thickened cream

Mix the fruit pulp with the lemon and orange juice.
Place the sugar and water in a pan and stir over a gentle heat until dissolved. Bring to the boil and boil for 5 minutes without stirring. Leave to cool.
Add the cold sugar syrup to the fruit mixture. Whip the cream until it is just thick and fold into the fruit mixture. Transfer to a freezer tray and freeze until firm.
Serves 6–8

Ice fruit brulée

2 bananas, peeled and sliced
juice ½ lemon
2 cups cream, whipped
few drops vanilla essence
1 pear, peeled, cored and chopped
1 peach, skinned, stoned and chopped
100 g black grapes, seeded and sliced
100 g soft brown sugar

Sprinkle the bananas with the lemon juice.
Whip the cream until thick, add the vanilla essence and stir in all the chopped fruits. Place in a shallow ovenproof dish and freeze.
Sprinkle the frozen dish with brown sugar and flash under a hot grill until the sugar caramelises. Serve immediately.
Serves 4–6
Note: To make this dessert even more delicious you can flavour the cream with a liqueur such as Cointreau or crème de cassis.

Peach and almond tart

350 g sweet shortcrust pastry
2 tablespoons butter
¼ cup sugar
⅜ cup ground almonds
4 tablespoons flour
2 egg yolks
2 drops almond essence
⅔ cup sugar
1¼ cups water
6 whole white peaches, peeled and stoned
2 tablespoons raspberry jelly
1 teaspoon cornflour
½ cup water
2 egg whites
¼ cup caster sugar
pinch salt
⅜ cup toasted flaked almonds

Roll out the dough and line a 20 cm flan case. Preheat oven to 200°C (400°F).
Cream the butter, sugar and ground almonds. Blend in the flour, egg yolks and almond essence. Fill the flan evenly with the almond paste and bake for 20 minutes on the middle shelf. Allow to cool.
Meanwhile, boil the sugar and water to a syrup and poach the peaches in it very gently for 10 minutes. Remove peaches, arrange them in the flan and keep the peach syrup for the next step.
Make a glaze by melting the raspberry jelly in 150 mL of the peach syrup. Mix the cornflour with the water and add to the melted jam. Cook for 3 minutes until glossy and pour over the peaches.
Beat the egg whites until stiff. Add the salt and half the sugar, beat until stiff, and repeat. Pipe the meringue between the peaches and scatter over the toasted flaked almonds. Put the dish under the grill for 1 minute to brown the meringue and serve immediately.
Serves 8

STRAWBERRY FLAN

1 Place the rolled out dough onto the flan case. Make a tuck of dough inside the case then cut off the extra dough.

2 Raise the tuck about 5 mm above the flan case.

3 Using tweezers or a fork, flute the raised edge for decoration.

4 Prick the base of the pastry case with a fork before baking.

Strawberry flan

225 g sweet shortcrust
1 egg yolk
225 g strawberries
1 tablespoon redcurrant jam

Glaze:
2 tablespoons redcurrant or strawberry jam
2 tablespoons sugar
50 mL water
1½ tablespoons cornflour

Roll out the dough 5 mm thick. Lift the dough on to the rolling pin and place on a 20 cm flan case on a greased baking sheet. Make an extra tuck of dough with your fingers all round. Then use the pressure of the rolling pin to cut off the extra dough.

Raise the tuck 5 mm above the flan case with your fingers and, using tweezers, make flutes as decoration.

Preheat the oven to 190°C (375°F). Prick the flan all over with a fork. Line with greaseproof paper, fill with rice and bake blind for 20 minutes.

Remove paper and rice, brush sides with beaten egg yolk and return to the oven for 5 minutes until a deep golden colour. Cool.

Spread the base with redcurrant jam.

Gently rinse the strawberries and drain on absorbent paper. Starting from the middle of the flan, arrange the strawberries in circles.

To make the glaze: boil the redcurrant jam, sugar and water in a saucepan. Mix the cornflour with a little water and add to the saucepan. Stir for 2 minutes until the glaze clears. While it is hot, brush it on to the flan. If using strawberry jam, strain before pouring on to the flan. Cool.

Serves 8

Basic pancakes

It has been the custom to leave pancake batter to stand for a while before cooking but experiments have shown that this makes very little difference to the final results. Cooked pancakes will keep for a week if wrapped in greaseproof paper and stored in the refrigerator. They can also be frozen. Reheat the pancakes in a lightly greased hot pan, turning once.

1⅛ cups flour
½ teaspoon salt
1 egg
1¼ cups milk
oil for frying

Sieve the flour and salt into a bowl. Add the egg and half the milk and beat thoroughly until smooth. Mix in the remaining milk and beat until bubbly.

Put the oil for frying in a heatproof jug. Pour a little of the oil into a 15cm frying pan over a fairly high heat. Tilt the pan to coat with oil, then pour any excess back into the jug.

When the pan is hot pour in a little batter, tilting the pan to thinly coat the base. Cook quickly, shaking the pan and loosening the edge with a palette knife until the underside is golden-brown. Toss the pancake and cook the second side.

Slide the cooked pancake out on to a plate and keep warm, covered with a second plate. Repeat with the remaining batter, to make 8–10 pancakes.

Fold the pancakes into quarters and serve with jam.

Serves 4

Pear and apple pancakes

1 quantity basic pancake batter
1 teaspoon cinnamon
2 red apples
3 pears
¼ cup sugar
1 tablespoon cornflour
juice 1 orange
3 tablespoons apricot jam
sugar for sprinkling

Make up the pancake batter adding the cinnamon with the flour. Make the pancakes following the instructions for the basic pancake recipe. Pile flat and keep warm between two plates while making the filling.

Quarter the apples and pears, remove cores and cut the fruit into chunks.

Place the sugar in a pan with 1¼ cups cold water and stir over a low heat until dissolved. Blend the cornflour with the orange juice and stir into the pan with the apricot jam. Bring to the boil and simmer for 3 minutes, stirring continuously.

Put some of the filling in the middle of each pancake, roll up and transfer to a heated serving dish. Sprinkle with a little sugar and serve.

Serves 4

Pear and apple pancakes

Nutty apple cake

Nutty apple cake

2¼ cups flour
2 teaspoons baking powder
¼ teaspoon salt
3 tablespoons margarine
2 tablespoons sugar
1 egg
⅝ cup milk
2 tablespoon butter
3 tablespoons soft brown sugar
¼ teaspoon cinnamon
¼ teaspoon nutmeg
450 g cooking apples
¼ cup demerara sugar
⅔ cup chopped nuts

Preheat the oven to 180°C (350°F).

Sieve the flour, baking powder and salt into a bowl. Rub in the margarine and stir in the sugar.

Beat the egg with the milk and stir into the flour to form a soft dough.

Combine the butter with the brown sugar and spices and spread over the base of a 27 × 18 cm shallow cake tin.

Peel, quarter, core and thinly slice the apples and arrange over the spicy mixture. Pat out the dough and place it over the apples, pressing it into the corners of the tin.

Bake in the preheated oven for 45 minutes, then turn on to a wire rack.

Mix together the demerara sugar and chopped nuts and sprinkle on top of the cake while it is still warm. Allow to cool completely.

Serves 6–8

One-stage Victoria sandwich cake

Delicious creamed butter sponges have a high proportion of fat and sugar to flour and are quite rich. To prevent curdling of the cake mixture, eggs should be at room temperature before you add them to the butter and sugar. Flat on top and an appetising golden colour the classic butter sponge lends itself to generous icings and fillings.

½ cup butter or margarine
½ cup caster sugar
2 large eggs
1 teaspoon baking powder
1⅛ cups self-raising flour
1 cup cream, whipped
⅜ cup strawberry jam
1 tablespoon icing sugar

Preheat the oven to 170°C (325°F). Place the butter or margarine, sugar, eggs, baking powder and flour in a bowl and beat well with a wooden spoon until mixture is airy and smooth.

Divide the mixture between 2 greased and lined 18 cm sandwich tins and bake on the middle shelf of the oven for 25–35 minutes. Meanwhile, whip the cream.

Turn the cakes out on a rack to cool and remove the lining. Sandwich the cake with a layer of jam and then a layer of whipped cream. Dust the top with icing sugar.

Serves 6–8

Lemon sponge

ingredients for Victoria sandwich cake
rind 1 lemon, grated
½ cup butter or margarine
1⅔ cups icing sugar
1 tablespoon lemon juice
few strips angelica

Make the cake following instructions for Victoria sandwich cake but add the lemon rind to the sugar and butter mixture at the time you add the beaten eggs.

Place the butter or margarine in a basin and gradually beat in the icing sugar. Continue to beat until the mixture is smooth and light. Add the lemon juice and mix to a soft spreading consistency.

Use a little of this lemon cream to sandwich the two cake halves. Spread more over the top and decorate with parallel ridges made by moving a round-tipped knife over the cream. Fill a piping bag fitted with a star nozzle with the remaining lemon cream and pipe swirls around the rim. Decorate with angelica in the shape of leaves and serve.

Serves 6–8

Lemon sponge

Caramel cream gateau

Caramel cream gateau

1 basic sponge, cut in half
2 tablespoons sugar
1 tablespoon water
1¼ cups cream
1 cup almonds, flaked and toasted

Place the sugar and water in a pan and stir over a low heat until dissolved. Increase the heat and boil rapidly until it is a light caramel colour. Remove from the heat and immediately stir in 2 tablespoons of the cream. Allow to become cold.

Add the remaining cream to the caramel and whip until thick. Use to sandwich the sponges and to spread over the top and sides of the cake. Sprinkle the cake with the almonds or garnish imaginatively to your taste.

Serves 4–6

Index

Anchovy and garlic stuffed eggs 23
Apricot stuffing 60
Apricot whip 86
Artichoke hearts 20
Asparagus au gratin 64
Asparagus sauce 16
Avocado grill 19

bacon garnish 7
Baked fish with parsley rice 82
Banana mousse 85
Banana rum bavarois 85
Barramundi provençale 30
Basic household stock 7
Basic pancakes 92
Béarnaise sauce 14
Béchamel sauce 16
    variations Asparagus sauce 16
              Mushroom sauce 16
beef
    see Burgundy beef 38
         Roast beef 37
         Sirloin with peppercorns 38
         Steak and kidney pie 42
Beef and carrot soup 9
Beef and eggplant pie 41
Beef goulash 41
Bolognese sauce and spaghetti 73
Bouquet garni 7
Braised veal in mushroom sauce 47
Brandy and orange pancakes 27
Broccoli in caper sauce 64
Burgundy beef 38

Cannelloni with olives 75
Cantaloup hors d'oeuvre 20
Caramel cream gâteau 95
Cauliflower and macaroni soufflé 77
Celery mornay 63
Cheese and onion quiches 26
chicken
    see Country chicken risotto 78
         Cream of chicken soup 12
         Deep-fried chicken balls 27
         Farmhouse potato and chicken casserole 55
         Provençal chicken 56
         Tandoori chicken 59
         Walnut chicken 55
Chicken liver kebabs 61
Chicken tarragon 59
Chicken with olives and mushrooms 56
Chilled mushroom and lemon soup 12
Chinese sausage pancakes 26
Chinese spare ribs 45
Citrus sherbet cups 87
Country chicken risotto 78
Crab and raisin salad 69
Cream of chicken soup 12
Cream of lettuce soup 12
Cream of mushroom soup 10
Crème caramel 85
croûtes 7
croûtons 7
Crown roast of pork 48
Curried brown rice salad 82

Deep fried chicken balls 27
Dolmades 78
duck *see* Roast duckling 59
dumplings or meatballs 7

Egg and anchovy mousse 24

Farmhouse potato and chicken casserole 55
Flemish pork with red cabbage 50
Frankfurts and noodles 77
French onion soup 9
Fresh fruit ice-cream 90
Fresh tomato soup 13

Giblet gravy 9

Herb butter 17
herbs and greens garnish 7
Hollandaise sauce 14
Horseradish sauce 17

Iced fruit brulée 90
Italian-style pork chops 50

John Dory *see* Shallow-fried John Dory 30

lamb *see* Norfolk parcel 46
        Shoulder of lamb with apricot and pawpaw sauce 45
        Stuffed leg of lamb 42
Lamb Louise 45
Lasagne al Forno 74
Leatherjacket with green anchovy butter 32
Lemon sponge 94
Lime trifle 88
Lobster gratiné 34

Macaroni and zucchini salad 71
Melba toast 7
Mixed vegetable soup 10
Moules marinières 35
Mulligatawny 10
Mushroom flan 68
Mushroom garnish 7
Mushroom sauce 16

Norfolk parcel 46
Nutty apple cake 93

One-stage Victoria sandwich cake 94
Onions in cream sauce 68
Osso buco with artichoke hearts 47
Oysters Rockefeller 34

pancakes
    see Brandy and orange pancakes 27
        Chinese sausage pancakes 26
        Pear and apple pancakes 92
pasta garnish 7
Pasta shepherd's pie 42
Peach and almond tart 90
Pear and apple pancakes 92
Pineapple flambé 88
pork
    see Crown roast of pork 48
        Flemish pork with red cabbage 50
        Italian-style pork chops 50
Pork casserole 52
Portuguese sauce 14
Potato and celery salad 71
Potato and onion stuffing 60
Prawn rissoles 20
Prawns with bean sprouts 35
Provençal chicken 56

quiche *see* Cheese and onion quiches 26

Raspberry soufflé 87
Rice pilaff 78
Roast beef 37
Roast duckling 59
    Apricot stuffing for 60
    Potato and onion stuffing for 60

Rum and chocolate mousse 86
Sausage and vegetable casserole 53
seafood garnishes 29
Seafood hors d'oeuvre 24
Shallow-fried John Dory 30
Shoulder of lamb with apricot and pawpaw sauce 45
Silver bream with basil 32
sippets 7
Sirloin with peppercorns 38
Snapper Mexicana 32
spaghetti *see* Bolognese sauce with spaghetti 73
Spaghetti Amalfi 74
Spanish seafood paella 81
Spanish turkey casserole 60
Spinach turnovers 69
Spring onion butter 17
Springtime salad 71
Steak and kidney pie 42
Stir-fried chicken with bamboo shoots 56
stock *see* Basic household stock 7
Strawberry de luxe 86
Strawberry flan 91
Stuffed leg of lamb 42
Stuffed vine leaves 67

Tandoori chicken 59
Taramasalata 19
Tartare sauce 14
Tomato pie 67
Tomato sauce 14
Tomatoes Roquefort 69
Tomatoes stuffed with rice 81
Trout meunière 30
Tuna bread 23
turkey *see* Spanish turkey casserole 60

veal *see* Osso buco with artichoke hearts 47
Veal escalopes in marsala 47
Vichyssoise 13

Walnut chicken 55

Yorkshire pudding 37

Printed in Singapore